Queen Victoria's Scotland

Queen Victoria's Scotland

MICHAEL J. STEAD

Introduction by
THEO ARONSON

CASSELL

A CASSELL BOOK

First published in the UK 1992
by Cassell
Villiers House
41/47 Strand
LONDON
WC2N 5JE

Format © 1992 Cassell
Photography & Text © 1992 Michael J. Stead
Introduction © 1992 Theo Aronson

Distributed in Australia
by Capricorn Link (Australia) Pty Ltd
P.O. Box 665, Lane Cove, NSW 2066

CIP data is available upon request from
the British Library National Bibliographic Service

ISBN 0-304-34105-3

'Frontispiece: . . . *we
could just see* Kilchurn
Castle *of historic
celebrity, and the
beautiful head of the
loch with high hills to
the right.'*

Typeset by Litho Link Limited, Welshpool, Powys

Printed and bound in Great Britain by
Bath Colourbooks, Scotland

Contents

'This Mixture of Great Wildness and Art is Perfection'

Queen Victoria

Acknowledgements

O N such a major project as this, progress to a successful conclusion would not be possible without a great deal of assistance from various sources. Each made the work involved possible or easier, for which I am grateful.

My most sincere thanks must be expressed to the Royal Household for their kind permission to allow the reproduction of the *Journal* extracts and line illustrations, without which there would have been no publication.

Time is always an important factor with anything involving the landscape, particularly when deadlines are short and the weather is British. Twice I had to resort to a vehicle where normally I would have walked. In both cases, it was necessary to drive along tracks normally prohibited to vehicles and I am grateful for the special permissions granted from those estates concerned: Invercauld for the Glen Callater track and Inchrory for the Glen Avon to Loch Builg track. In the latter instance, I owe especial thanks to the owner, Sir Seton Wills, not only for the permission but also for his kind personal suggestions on how best to negotiate the terrain when I was fortunate enough to meet him on site!

I would also like to thank Dave Gadd in Scarborough for the careful processing of the colour transparency film, and Dave Gray of Walker's Studios, Scarborough, for allowing me access to his darkroom so that I could print the black-and-white work personally.

Finally, but certainly not least, I would like to thank Lorraine for all her assistance throughout this project: sharing the driving, walking (and soakings), map reading, itinerary planning etc, but mostly for being there, when as inevitably happens 'the best laid schemes . . . gang aft a-gley', to give moral support, tea (when the gas keg wasn't empty), sympathy and understanding.

Author's Preface

I FIRST came across Queen Victoria's *Leaves from the Journal of Our Life in the Highlands* and its sequel, *More Leaves from the Journal of a Life in the Highlands*, whilst undertaking research for another book entitled *Literary Landscapes*. For this I needed passages of literature, poems, or extracts from journals which described an aspect of, or location within, the landscape of the British Isles. When an acquaintance remarked that he had once read a compilation of diary entries describing the Scottish Highlands written by Queen Victoria, I thought that this might prove a suitable source of material.

Initially, I intended to include one or possibly two *Journal* extracts which, like the other extracts for the project, would each be accompanied by a single photograph. However, the more I read, the more I became immersed in the wonderful descriptive narrative, and I realized that the *Journals* alone could spur me to produce enough photographic material for a completely new publication.

When deciding on the structure of this book my main concern was the photography, but I also wanted to produce more than just a series of Scottish scenes. I wanted to illustrate the particular charms and moods of the country which so endeared itself to the Queen; and which were responsible for persuading her to record these strong emotions for posterity. At the same time I hoped to complement an already superb text; a task made easier for me by the fact that I too find the starkness, richness and power of these particular landscapes an irresistible magnet to my camera lens.

As space dictated that I could not reproduce and illustrate both *Journals* in their entirety I had to be quite ruthless in my final selection – based on topography – to ensure that the final book would be truly representative of the extensive travels of Her Majesty. After that the criterion was simply that, within each defined area, I would choose those passages which best displayed Queen Victoria's excellent powers of observation and, through the descriptive narrative, conveyed her intense love for the Scottish landscape.

As a contrast, those descriptions from her record of life on the Balmoral estate have been chosen specifically to show that this emotional involvement extended beyond the landscape of the Highlands to its people also, particularly her employees and their families, whose life-styles were a constant source of interest to the Queen, and whose tragedies were shared with the compassion and care expected more of a relative than an employer who was also the ruler of the British Empire.

With material of the quality found in the *Journals*, there were bound to be problems regarding selection. Although, in my view, the final choice was the most suitable, on more than one occasion I was forced to exclude an entry which would have warranted inclusion if space had permitted. Nowhere was the difficulty more pronounced than with those passages relating to the mountainous regions around Balmoral. In her time, Queen Victoria actually reached the majority of the summits immediately north and south of the estate. For this era, these feats were exceptional, displaying the Queen's amazing courage and sense of adventure, and her narratives would put many of today's so-called guide-writers to shame. Consequently, apart from Lochnager, which obviously selected itself, the account of the ascent of Ben Macdui is included because it represents probably the most difficult and strenuous of all these particular excursions, and perhaps illustrates the tremendous nerve of the Queen, assuming she had heard the legend of The Great White One who stalks its slopes. However in no way is the account literarily superior to those of other ascents which regrettably were excluded.

Michael J. Stead

Introduction

by Theo Aronson

Queen Victoria, on her own admission, was 'naturally very passionate'. And one of the most intense of her passions was for Scotland. 'I cannot describe,' she once protested, 'how beautiful it is.' She nevertheless went on, with a wealth of underlinings, capital letters and exclamation marks, to do exactly that. It was, she claimed, 'the most enchanting' country in the world and one which she was proud to call her own. Its landscape was so 'wild and romantic'; its atmosphere so 'sublime and impressive'; its people so 'shrewd, clever, noble, very independent and proud in their bearing'. Balmoral Castle, her Highland home, was simply 'a Paradise'. Beside the delights of this 'glorious, blessed place', England was depressingly 'tame, dull and formal'.

Can one wonder that her children's governess, Lady Lyttleton, should complain of the Queen's insistence that 'Scotch air, Scotch people, Scotch hills, Scotch rivers, Scotch woods are all preferable to those of any other nation in or out of this world'? Or that her ex-Prime Minister, Lord Melbourne, should check her exuberant extolling of the virtues of the country with the wry observation that there was nothing to detract from the beauty of Scotland, 'except the very high opinion that the Scotch themselves entertain of it'.

For Queen Victoria, it was love at first sight. She and her

husband, Prince Albert, both 23 years old, first visited Scotland in September 1842. They had sailed up the east coast, landing at Leith, and visited Edinburgh, Perth, Taymouth and Stirling. In no time, the royal pen was detailing the country's myriad attractions. It was all so delightfully different: Edinburgh was 'quite beautiful, totally unlike anything else I have seen'; the children, with their flowing red hair and bare feet, were extraordinarily handsome; the hills were all so richly wooded, the mountains so spectacular, the castles so picturesque, the waterfalls so impressive, the lochs so vast, the songs of the Gaelic boatmen 'so wild and singular'.

Hardly less singular was the fact that Queen Victoria was visiting Scotland at all. Except for a short stay by King George IV in 1822, no reigning British monarch had set foot in the country for over two centuries. The Jacobite uprisings of the eighteenth century, in which the mainly Scottish adherents of the House of Stuart had rebelled against the House of Hanover to which Queen Victoria belonged, had resulted in a legacy of ill-feeling between England and Scotland. In Scotland, memories of the Old and Young Pretenders, of the massacre of the Highlanders at the battle of Culloden and of the brutal 'clearances' of the clansmen from their land in the years that followed, were still vivid. To the Queen's effusions on the romance and picturesqueness of the clans, Lord Melbourne's reply was characteristically cynical: 'What a good thing, considering their history of insurrection against the Hanoverian monarchy, that there were so few clans left.'

It is some measure, then, of her complete identification with Scotland that Queen Victoria (in whose own veins Stuart blood ran very thin indeed) could claim, 30 years after her first visit, that *she* was now the representative of the Stuart dynasty and that 'the people are as devoted and loyal to me, as they were to that unhappy race'.

The Queen's second visit came two years after her first. Again the royal couple sailed up the east coast, disembarking at Dundee, from where they drove to Blair Castle where they spent several weeks. The Queen's reactions were no less ecstatic. Much of her enthusiasm was due to the fact that her adored husband, Prince Albert, was equally enamoured of the country. It reminded him of parts of his native Germany. 'Albert in such delight,' she wrote from Blair Castle in September 1844, 'it is a happiness to see him, he is in such spirits . . . he is in ecstasies here.' There was, they agreed, 'a great peculiarity about the Highlands and Highlanders' and, the spectacular scenery apart,

'Loch Laggan . . . is a beautiful lake (small in comparison to what we had seen) surrounded by very fine mountains.'

'The moment you step out of the house [Blair Castle] you see those splendid hills all round.'

there was 'a quiet, a retirement, a wildness, a liberty, and a solitude that had such a charm for us'.

The couple came again in 1847. This time they toured the west coast. Not even the rain, which fell almost continuously, could dampen the Queen's spirits. Their chief delight in Ardverikie, the house on Loch Laggan in which they eventually established themselves, was that it was, as Prince Albert put it, 'an un-come-at-able place'. For this, more and more, was what the royal couple were coming to appreciate. Already, to get away from the pressures of officialdom at Buckingham Palace and Windsor, and to lead a more informal life with their growing family (by 1847 the couple had five children; they were to have four more), they had found themselves a home on the Isle of Wight.

But not even there, at Osborne House, could they be as isolated as they would have liked. In spite of the frequently choppy waters of the Solent, Osborne House was still too accessible; they were always having their privacy disturbed by visiting ministers and officials. What they needed was something even more remote. Might not a home in Scotland – 600 miles from the seat of government – grant them more privacy?

While they were sitting in rain-soaked Ardverikie that autumn, they heard that in Aberdeenshire, a mere 45 miles across the Cairngorms, the sun was shining. This startling information came in letters from their doctor's son, at that time a guest of Sir Robert Gordon, the tenant of a little castle beside the River Dee, known as Balmoral. As their doctor was forever extolling the virtues of upper Deeside as one of the driest and best-drained areas of Scotland, the royal couple, on their return to England, began thinking in terms of acquiring a home there.

And then, a few weeks after their return, they heard that Sir Robert Gordon had dropped dead at the breakfast table at Balmoral. There and then, and sight unseen, they decided to take up the lease of the property.

By the following year, 1848, Victoria and Albert were in possession of a Highland home.

* * *

Until the couple could buy the Balmoral estate and build a home of their own, they lived in the existing castle. From the time of their first stay, in September 1848, they spent every autumn at Balmoral; after Prince Albert's death in 1861, the Queen was to extend her stay from late August to late November, and then add a late-spring holiday. Eventually she would be spending over a third of each year in the '*dear*, beautiful Highlands'.

Balmoral Castle from the south-east.

'Loch Inch . . . *is not a wild lake, quite the contrary, no high rocks, but woods and blue hills as a background.'*

'. . . we came to a very extraordinary Roman encampment at Ardoch, *called the 'Lindrum'. Albert got out; but I remained in the carriage, and Major Moray showed it to him. They say it is one of the most perfect in existence.'*

Her first view of Balmoral fulfilled all her expectations. Although the castle was small, it was very pretty, and the setting was, she said, the finest she had ever seen. It was 'very wild and solitary and yet cheerful and *beautifully wooded*'. One felt that one could walk, she reported to her Uncle Leopold, King of the Belgians, for ever. She seldom walked for less than four hours a day and, the minute she got back, she felt like setting out again. 'And then the wildness, the solitariness of everything is so delightful, so refreshing,' she continued. 'The people are so good and simple – and uncivilised, though well educated.'

Indeed, it was by the Highlanders, as much as by the Highlands, that Queen Victoria was so taken. A shy woman, in spite of holding what she herself called 'the greatest position there is', the Queen was never really at ease in aristocratic or intellectual society. She always felt more relaxed among the poor and the unsophisticated. And the people with whom she came in contact on the Balmoral estate – the crofters, gillies and tenants – all seemed to be such admirable people: natural without being uncouth, proud without being arrogant, respectful without being obsequious. They were never afraid to look one in the eye, to say what was on their minds, to do as they pleased. The old women whom she visited in their cottages were so full of commonsense; the men who led her ponies so full of shrewd observations.

And then, with her eye for masculine good looks, Queen Victoria greatly admired the strong physique and proud bearing of the Highland men. At the Highland Games at Braemar Castle, which the royal family attended each year, she would make appreciative note of the virility of the men as, wearing only shirts and kilts and invariably in an icy wind, they ran their races, threw their hammers and tossed their cabers.

The annual Braemar Gathering was part of a movement to preserve and promote Highland culture. It was a movement into which Queen Victoria flung herself with customary gusto. She insisted on the wearing of the kilt by all the men of the household, including Prince Albert; she invariably flung a plaid shawl over her shoulders; her children were kitted out in 'Highland things' which they passed down one to another, irrespective of gender. The family started to learn Gaelic, to dance reels, to appreciate the pipes.

Indeed, it was Queen Victoria's new-found passion for all things Scottish that helped popularize Highland dress. Until comparatively recently, the wearing of Scottish national dress had not been particularly widespread; the early nineteenth-century interest in it had been confined to the upper and middle classes, partly due to their reading of the novels of Sir Walter Scott. Ordinary Highlanders still tended to wear breeches instead of kilts. But Queen Victoria's enthusiasm ensured that Highland dress became far more generally worn. And not only in Scotland; throughout the British Empire little boys and girls were soon sporting the 'Highland things' as worn by Victoria and Albert's children.

Prince Albert's identification with the country was no less wholehearted. To his wife's various enthusiasms he added one of his own – for hunting. A dedicated sportsman, the Prince was soon adept at stalking, the most customary method of taking deer in Scotland. At the end of the day's sport, in true Highland tradition, the stags would be laid out at the door of the castle and, after dinner, the Queen, in evening dress and tiara, would come out to be shown the dead game by her husband.

Victoria and Albert were both, of course, very interested in drawing and painting, and many artists were commissioned to capture the scenes of their life in the Highlands. Painters such as William Leitch, James Giles, Carl Haag and, pre-eminently, Edwin Landseer were kept busy recording the landscapes, castles, picnics, hunts and expeditions that went to make up the varied delights of their Scottish holidays. Occasions like the laying of the last stone by Prince Albert on the cairn on Craig Gowan, in October 1852 (an event celebrated by the downing of

'After breakfast Albert saw Lord Glenlyon, who proposed that he should go deerstalking'

an inordinate amount of whisky: the people, noted the Queen gamely, were 'wild with excitement'), were dutifully recorded.

The diarist Charles Greville, visiting Balmoral in his capacity of Clerk of the Privy Council, grudgingly admitted that the royal couple were at their best in this relatively simple setting. He was particularly struck by Prince Albert's many admirable qualities. Regarding him, until this Balmoral visit, as a pedantic and censorious German, Greville now came to appreciate not only his intelligence and quick comprehension, but his informality and high spirits. Scotland, in short, was bringing out the best in Prince Albert.

The royal couple always dreaded their return south. 'I was *quite* miserable to leave these fine, wild mountains, that pure air,' she wrote on one day of departure. And, on another, when she woke to find everything covered in snow, she longed to be snowed in. How happy that would have made her, she sighed. 'I *pine* for my dear Highlands which I get more attached to every year,' she once wrote from Windsor to her half-sister Féodore, Princess of Hohenlohe-Langenburg. 'The life here is *so* different; it is so formal to what it is there!' She then went on to quote an early Byron poem:

> England! thy beauties are tame and domestic
> To one who has roved o'er the Mountains afar;
> Oh for the Crags that are wild and majestic!
> The steep frowning glories of dark Loch na Gar!

*　*　*

In 1852, Victoria and Albert were able to buy the Balmoral estate and, four years later, with the final destruction of the previous castle, the entire household moved into the new Balmoral Castle. Designed by the Scots architect, William Smith, working under the direction of Prince Albert, it was sited 100 yards north-west of the original building, thus affording even finer views along the River Dee. That the castle, which was the private property of the royal couple, could have been envisaged on quite so impressive a scale was due to the fact that the Queen had recently been bequeathed the sum of ½ million pounds by an eccentric old bachelor.

The new building, with its massive central tower, its pale granite walls, its pepperpot turrets, its battlements and stepped gables, was a mixture of German *schloss* and Scottish baronial hall. Built to accommodate no less than 100 people (the much-vaunted 'simplicity' of Queen Victoria's life in the Highlands was relative, and room had always to be found for guests and government ministers), it boasted the hitherto unheard-of luxury of four bathrooms and 14 water-closets.

Whatever its exterior style, its decor within was uncompromisingly Scottish. With her new-found passion for tartan, the Queen lavished it on her apartments. The carpets would be one tartan, the curtains another, the furniture upholstered in a third. Tartan cloths would be flung over tables; tartan rugs scattered on the floors. Where the paper covering the walls did not feature tartan, it would feature thistles. To what has been described as the 'tartanitis' of the rooms, the Queen contributed still more by wearing tartan dresses and tartan shawls and by ensuring that all the Highlanders in her service wore Stuart tartan. Prince Albert even designed their own Balmoral tartan: a design of lilac, red and black on a grey background.

But the Scottishness of the decor did not end with the use of tartan. In the drawing-room, the four-branched candelabra were held aloft by Highlanders carved in Parian marble. Where stags' heads were not jutting from the walls, their antlers would be fashioned into chairs and settles. Almost every picture depicted scenes from the Queen's life in the Highlands. Even the Scottish-born Lady Augusta Bruce had to admit that although the decoration was 'characteristic and appropriate', it was hardly *flatteuse* to the eye.

Can one be surprised that Lord Rosebery once remarked that he had always imagined the drawing-room at Osborne to be the ugliest in the world until he saw the drawing-room at Balmoral?

But to Queen Victoria, it was perfection. These 'cheerful and unpalace-like rooms' were exactly what she wanted. And if ever she felt the need of something even more cheerful and unpalace-like, there was always the cottage on the estate, known as Alt-na-Giuthasach, where only the Queen, the Prince, a maid-of-honour and a handful of servants could live in complete seclusion.

In addition to planning the castle, the industrious Prince Albert had been planning the grounds. He bought, or leased, adjoining properties; he planted trees, marked out new roads and paths, laid out formal gardens, drained and trenched wasteland, built new cottages and outhouses. A ballroom was added to the castle. Within its mock-Gothic interior, lavishly decorated in the 'ancient Scottish' style, the gillies would enjoy their annual ball. To the amount of whisky downed at this yearly romp, the Queen turned a blind eye. Censorious in so many ways, Victoria was exceptionally tolerant when it came to the excessive drinking of

'We drove to above Slatterdale, where there is such a splendid view of the loch [Loch Maree] and of Ben Sleach; and the hills looked so beautifully pink'.

'It is a walk of three miles round, and a very steep ascent; at every turn the view of the rushing falls [of Bruar] is extremely fine'.

Balmoral Castle
from the north-west.

the Highlanders. She would often note, without a hint of disapproval, that this or that retainer was 'too bashful' – too drunk – to carry out his duties.

So, all in all, Queen Victoria could hardly have been more delighted with her Scottish home. 'Every year,' she wrote in the autumn during which they finally moved into the new castle, 'my heart becomes more fixed in this dear Paradise, and so much more so now that *all* has become my dearest Albert's *own* creation, own work, own building, own laying out . . . and his great taste, and the impress of his dear hand, have been stamped everywhere.'

* * *

Although Balmoral was meant to serve as a retreat from political life, it was here that one of the royal couple's most cherished political schemes was set in train. This was a proposed future alliance between Britain and a Prussian-led Germany.

Victoria and Albert looked forward to the day when the fragmented and despotically-ruled states of Germany would be united into a single democratic country. The lead for such a movement would have to come from the most dynamic of these states, Prussia. But as Prussia was no less despotically ruled, it would be up to Britain to guide her along a more liberal path. Injected with British liberalism, Prussia could set about liberalizing and unifying Germany.

As a first step towards this high-minded goal, Victoria and

Albert decided on a link between the royal houses of Britain and Prussia. Fortunately there were two eminently suitable candidates to hand. The one was Prince Frederick Wilhelm of Prussia; the other was their eldest daughter Vicky, the Princess Royal. Prince Frederick Wilhelm, known as Fritz, was a tall, handsome, good-natured young man with progressive views; Vicky was pretty and precocious, something of a prodigy.

So, in the autumn of 1855, when Fritz was 24 years old and Vicky a mere 14, Victoria and Albert invited the Prussian prince to Balmoral. Everything went as planned. Within four days Fritz had made up his mind. After breakfast the following morning, he asked the parents for their daughter's hand. They agreed, with the proviso that he wait for several months before proposing. But quite clearly no one was in a mood for waiting and, four days later, Fritz spoke to Vicky. As the royal party were riding their ponies up the slopes of Craig-na-Ban, he picked Vicky a sprig of white heather; as they were riding down, he declared his love.

Once they were all back at the castle, Vicky rushed into her mother's room to tell her the news. Victoria was ecstatic. Quite clearly this was a love match, as her own had been. And how appropriate that this 'happy conclusion' had been reached in her beloved Scotland.

The young couple were married in 1858. And although Fritz was eventually to become Emperor of a united Germany, it would not be the liberal state of Victoria and Albert's – and of his and Vicky's – fond hopes. But in memory, perhaps, of the optimistic dawn of the scheme, Fritz was always to treasure the Highland dress which Queen Victoria had presented to him. His eldest son, the future Kaiser Wilhelm II, would recall with pleasure standing in his father's dressing-room, admiring 'the precious and glittering contents of his box of Highland clothes'.

* * *

What Queen Victoria probably appreciated most about Scotland was the scenery. In this, she was very much in tune with contemporary taste. Half a century before, its desolate moors and craggy peaks would have been considered far too savage. The rational eighteenth century had preferred a gentle landscape of rolling fields, clustered trees, ornamental lakes and Palladian villas. But by now, and for most of the period to which Queen Victoria was to give her name, the taste was for wilder, more romantic surroundings. Switzerland, with its lakes and mountains and waterfalls, was considered the ideal of nineteenth-century scenery.

'We drove through Fort William, *on as we did yesterday morning by* Achintee, *and down the eastern side of* Loch Eil, *which was beautifully lit, the distant hills intensely blue.'*

'Glen Derry, which is very fine, with the remnants of a splendid forest, Cairn Derry *being to the right, and the* Derry Water *running below. The track was very bad and stony.'*

'These Scotch streams, full of stones, and clear as glass, are most beautiful; the peeps between the trees, the depth of the shadows, the mossy stones, mixed with slate etc., which cover the banks, are lovely; at every turn you have a picture.'

*Sketch from 'Visit to the
Prince's Encampment
at Feithort'.*

Prince Albert, who had visited Switzerland and whose native Thuringia was not unlike Deeside, described Scotland as 'simply glorious', while Queen Victoria wrote, even more effusively, of her '*adoration*' for Mountains . . . There is nothing like Mountains, Mountain Scenery and Mountaineers'.

The couple spent as much time as possible out of doors. While Albert was out shooting, Victoria would be sketching or riding or driving. They loved setting out on day-long rides: scrambling up hillsides to view sites 'where the eagles sometimes sit'; fording ice-cold streams; picnicking in the heather; trailing home, often wet and exhausted, just as the sun was setting with 'the hills looking purple and lilac, most exquisite'.

An additional attraction for Queen Victoria was that at Balmoral, as opposed to Buckingham Palace, Windsor or even Osborne, she saw a great deal more of her adored husband. Although the marriage was never quite the unclouded idyll that she subsequently made it out to be, the couple were devoted to each other. Yet, away from Scotland, Prince Albert tended to behave towards her in a perfunctory, preoccupied fashion. He was, she once complained, 'a terrible man of business', involved in so many things from which she felt excluded. He worked far too hard. Although still only in his 30s throughout the 1850s, the Prince looked much older. Balding and paunchy, he had all the *gravitas* of a more mature man. He had never been strong and, by the end of the decade, was in an almost continuously depressed and harassed state, hardly able to cope with the strains of everyday living.

But once in Scotland, he was like a changed man: his cares seemed to fall away. These annual autumn holidays never failed to bring the couple great happiness and contentment. At

Balmoral they were able to enjoy, and demonstrate, the great love they felt for each other. For the rest of her long life, Victoria would always associate Scotland with the happiest times that she and her husband had spent together.

In September 1860 they embarked on the first of what the Queen called their 'Great Expeditions': a series of journeys in which they travelled, incognito, with a small suite, through some of the more remote parts of the country. By carriage, on horseback, on foot, they made their way through the roughest terrain and amongst the most spectacular scenery, sleeping in humble inns and eating simply cooked food.

Their identity seems never to have been guessed; although the crown emblazoned on the dog-cart might well have given things away. Now and then an attendant gillie might inadvertently call Victoria 'Your Majesty', and on one occasion a woman, seeing the many rings crammed onto the Queen's pudgy fingers, did remark that 'the lady must be terrible rich'.

The couple enjoyed four of these Great Expeditions and at the end of the fourth one, in October 1861, the Queen wrote, 'Alas, I fear our *last* great one'. By 'last' she meant the last great one of that year but, as things turned out, it was indeed to be the last one they enjoyed together. For almost exactly two months after this Great Expedition, on 14 December 1861, Prince Albert died.

* * *

Prince Albert's death crushed Queen Victoria. She was convinced that she would not long outlive him. Their separation, she felt sure, would '*not last* and those blessed Arms will receive me very shortly, *never* to part'. Yet far from following her husband to the grave, she still had half her life ahead of her. Together, husband and wife had visited Balmoral for 14 years; alone, Victoria would visit it for almost 40.

Her first return to Scotland, four months after Albert's death,

Sketch from the 'First Great Expedition' – the ferry across Loch Inch.

was almost unbearably painful. Together with two of her children, Princess Alice and Prince Alfred, and in pouring rain, she arrived at Balmoral on 2 May 1862. 'Oh! darling child,' she wrote to her eldest daughter Vicky, by now Crown Princess of Prussia, 'the agonising sobs as I crawled up with Alice and Affie! The stag's head – the rooms – blessed, darling Papa's room – then his coats – his caps – kilts – all, all convulsed my poor shattered frame!'

Having spent more time alone with Prince Albert at Balmoral than anywhere else, the Queen felt his absence more acutely. Her only solace was in paying pilgrimages to the places they had once visited and to planning memorials in his honour. She would visit the cairn on Craig Gowan and their cottage at Alt-na-Giuthasach. With six of her nine children she made her way to the top of Craig Lowrigan to lay the first stones of a projected pyramid in his honour. She ordered the erection of a memorial obelisk and commanded William Theed to fashion a huge bronze statue of the Prince in Highland dress. In Aberdeen she unveiled yet another statue of him. Determined to capture for posterity those Great Expeditions of 1860 and 1861, the Queen arranged for the painting of a series of watercolours depicting their various adventures.

And gradually, amidst the scenes in which she had once experienced such happiness, Victoria became more reconciled to her great loss. She was greatly helped by the attitude of her Highland retainers. All treated her sympathetically but sensibly. In 1862, on the anniversary of Prince Albert's birthday, John Grant, one of the most faithful of her gillies, chided her for treating it as a day of mourning. 'That's not the light to look at it,' he said. 'There is so much true and strong faith in these good simple people,' she commented.

And it is significant that it was in Scotland that the Queen gave the first indication of a renewed interest in life. By the autumn of 1863 – two years after Albert's death – she had resumed painting, and the artist William Leitch was able to report her as being cheerful and enjoying the work, 'chatting and occasionally laughing at the little difficulties and drawbacks'. On another occasion he wrote of 'lots of talking and laughing'; how quickly the time flew, remarked the Queen, when one was drawing.

Equally significant is the fact that when Queen Victoria was finally coaxed out of the depths of her depression it was by a Scotsman: by another of her Balmoral gillies, John Brown.

* * *

'. . . we went into Dornoch . . . quite a small place, but the capital of Sutherland, now much out of the world, as the railway does not go near it.'

'The view of Loch Vennachar, with the beautiful deep blue of Ben Venue and the other hills, was lovely.'

Queen Victoria had noticed the handsome young gillie soon after she and Prince Albert had first taken possession of Balmoral in 1848. In the years since then he had, by his skill, attentiveness and intelligence, developed into her most trusted outdoor servant. He had led her pony or been on the box of her carriage and had accompanied the Queen and the Prince on all their expeditions. Since Albert's death, Brown's unflustered behaviour during a couple of carriage accidents at Balmoral had confirmed the Queen's admiration for his skills, but it was not until the end of 1864 – three years after Prince Albert's death – that Brown began to assume a more significant role in her life.

The Queen was at Osborne that winter and, as her doctor was anxious for her to take up riding again, it was agreed that John Brown would be sent for. A strange groom, protested the Queen, would never do. So to Osborne came good, dependable, resourceful Brown.

From that time on, and for almost 20 years, John Brown was in close and constant attendance on Queen Victoria. As a woman who always needed masculine guidance and attention, the Queen came to rely, more and more, on Brown. Thirty-eight years old to her 45 in 1865, when he first became 'The Queen's Highland Servant', John Brown was the very epitome of the rude health and unashamed heartiness of the Highlander. His handsomeness was of a particularly Scots variety: he had clear blue eyes, a resolute chin and vigorously curling red-gold hair and beard. He always – even on the Queen's Continental holidays – wore the kilt. His personality, too, was what Victoria regarded as typically Scots. He had, she claimed, 'all the independence and elevated feelings peculiar to the Highland race, and is singularly

Mr. John Brown.

straight-forward, simple-minded [sic], kind-hearted and disinterested; always ready to oblige; and of a discretion rarely to be met with'.

Inevitably, the Queen's obsession with her gillie gave rise to scandal. Few could believe that their close association – those long solitary rides and walks on the Scottish hillsides, his constant attendance on her as she worked, the astonishing familiarity with which he addressed her – could be innocent. Rumours abounded. Some claimed that she had gone mad and that he was her keeper. Others believed that the link between them was psychic: that Queen Victoria was a spiritualist and that Brown – with his Scottish 'second sight' – was the medium through which she communed with the dead Prince Albert. Yet others said that he was her lover, and that she had had to go to Switzerland to bear his child. It was widely believed that he was her husband: in certain aristocratic circles, the Queen was always referred to as 'Mrs Brown'.

But John Brown was none of these things. To Queen Victoria, Brown was what so many members of a royal family lack – a friend. Although it may well have been his handsome masculinity that first attracted her, it was for his companionship that she came to value him so highly. As far as she was concerned, he was a disinterested and devoted companion, entirely dedicated to her interests. He was her protector, her supporter, her confidant; even, in his homespun way, her counsellor. Once the scandals had died down, Brown remained a permanent, accepted and very important part of Queen Victoria's life.

In Queen Victoria's eyes, John Brown personified all the virtues, all the pleasures, of her life in the Highlands.

* * *

A rather less controversial manifestation of Queen Victoria's love of Scotland came in 1868. In that year she published *Leaves from the Journal of Our Life in the Highlands*, an artless illustrated memoir of the holidays spent by the late Prince Albert and herself in their Scottish home. It was an immediate best-seller. Within months a cheaper 'people's edition' was published and, after that, a more lavish edition. Victoria attributed the book's success, in part, to the 'friendly footing' on which she lived with the Highlanders. 'Too friendly,' grumbled some members of her household. They resented the fact that in her book the Queen treated courtiers and servants alike; as though, complained one affronted lady-in-waiting, 'all are on the same footing'.

Victoria expected her children and grandchildren to share her unsnobbish attitude towards her Highland retainers. Arriving to stay at Balmoral, her grandchildren would always be sent, 'before anything else', to shake hands with the servants and gillies. When one of them refused to do any such thing, on the grounds that her mother had told her not to be too familiar with servants, the Queen was furious.

Leaves was followed, two years later, by the publication of two volumes of watercolour portraits, by Kenneth MacLeay, of various Scottish clansmen. The Queen had commissioned MacLeay to travel all over Scotland to paint the actual clansmen dressed in their authentic tartans. MacLeay had also depicted not only the Queen's three younger sons in Highland dress, but her favourite Balmoral retainers including, of course, John Brown. In MacLeay's flattering full-length portrait, Brown is shown as possessing all the distinction, assurance and elegance of a laird.

The Queen was also interesting herself in Scottish history. One year she visited Holyroodhouse, the Edinburgh palace where Mary, Queen of Scots had once lived, and made a characteristically thorough inspection of all the rooms in which that tragic Queen had spent some of her days. On another occasion she travelled through the Pass of Glen Coe, scene of what she called 'the bloody, fearful tale of woe' – the massacre of the unsuspecting MacDonalds by the Campbells. She went on to Loch Shiel, where 'a very ugly monument' marked the spot where Bonnie Prince Charlie landed in 1745 to rally the clans in favour of the Stuarts against the Hanoverians. 'I thought I never saw a lovelier or more romantic spot, or one which told its history so well. What a scene it must have been in 1745!' wrote Victoria. 'And here was *I*, the descendant of the Stuarts and of the very King whom Prince Charles sought to overthrow, sitting and walking about quite privately and peaceably.'

This was the occasion on which the Queen spoke of feeling 'a sort of reverence in going over these scenes in this most beautiful country, which I am proud to call my own, where there was such devoted loyalty to the family of my ancestors – for Stuart blood is in my veins, and I am *now* their representative'.

*   *   *

One day in October 1867, in pouring rain, Queen Victoria attended the unveiling of Theed's statue to Prince Albert at Balmoral. It was the twenty-eighth anniversary of their engagement day: 'a dear and sacred day'. Although, on occasions such as

'The scene of our drive to-day is all described in 'Rob Roy'. Loch Arklet lies like Loch Callater, only that the hills are higher and more pointed.'

this, the late Prince was still very much in her thoughts, the Queen was beginning to make her own decisions and not always to wonder what he might have done in similar circumstances. She was starting to live her own life. Already, in an effort to distance herself even further from the public gaze which she had come to hate so much, Victoria had taken possession of a little retreat in Glen Gelder. Called Gelder Shiel, it was a tiny, two-roomed cottage to which she added an inscription, in Gaelic, over the door, meaning 'The Queen's House'. Here, accompanied by the faithful Brown, she would often take tea.

And not only tea. One day, meeting Brown with a basket on his arm on his way to accompany the Queen on an outing, one of the maids-of-honour asked if it were tea that he was taking out. 'Wall, no,' replied Brown. 'She don't much like tea. We tak oot biscuits and sperruts.' He made the best cup of tea she had ever drunk, the Queen once told Brown. So it should be, he explained bluntly: he put 'a grand nip o' whisky' in it.

The Queen built another retreat ('a totally new house . . . my first Widow's house, not built by him or hallowed by his memory') called Glassalt Shiel. Set in another of those wild and picturesque spots on the shores of Loch Muick, but looking like nothing so much as a suburban villa, Glassalt Shiel became one of her favourite haunts. On the arm of John Brown, she would often walk along the lonely pebbled shore of the loch. She always returned from her stays there, noted her private secretary, 'much the better and livelier'.

She was also beginning to accept invitations to stay at great Scottish houses: with the Argylls at Inveraray, the Roxburghes at

View of Gelder Shiel.

'Dunrobin Castle . . .
has a very fine imposing
appearance with its
very high roof and
turrets, a mixture of
old Scotch castle and
French chateau.'

Floors, the Sutherlands at Dunrobin. At other times she would take possession of a house while the owners were away. One such stay was at Invertrossachs, as the Queen was anxious to explore the Trossachs, the beautiful glen immortalized in the books of Sir Walter Scott.

The rapid spread of the railway system not only made the journey up from London quicker and more convenient but allowed her to explore the whole of Scotland with an ease undreamed of in the days that she had first visited it with Prince Albert. The royal pen was tireless in detailing the many beauties of the places she was now able to visit: the slopes carpeted in pink and purple heather, the dramatic skies, the dark-blue hills, the ruined castles, the silvery mists, the tumbling burns, the densely wooded glens. All these, allied to the sterling qualities of the people, made 'beloved' Scotland, she once exclaimed, 'the proudest, finest country in the world'.

* * *

The tirelessness and enthusiasm with which Queen Victoria journeyed privately through Scotland was not echoed in the carrying-out of her public duties in England. There, to the despair of successive governments, she persisted in the guise of the broken-hearted widow whose solitary state and frail health would not allow for the leading of a more active public life.

In spite of the fact that the late-spring visit to Balmoral, which she had by now added to her annual autumn visit, took place during the Parliamentary session, Victoria was always adamant about not changing her dates of arrival or departure. Only a constitutional crisis of the most serious nature would induce her to alter her plans by perhaps a day or two. What she called her 'shattered nerves and health' could only find some solace, she would maintain, in Scotland.

Yet even here she could not entirely escape her constitutional obligations. She was forced to put up with a Minister in Attendance, often the Prime Minister. When this was the detested Gladstone (who thought nothing of a daily 25-mile walk at Balmoral), she would ensure that their time together was kept to a minimum: he was forever badgering her to emerge from her seclusion and make more effort. When it was her beloved Disraeli, she could scarcely see enough of him. Yet as much as Gladstone approved of the bracing qualities of the Highlands, so did Disraeli disapprove of them. It was all so bleak, so cold, so windswept. Privately, Disraeli grumbled about the difficulties of 'carrying on the government of a country six hundred miles from the metropolis'.

Never for a moment, though, did the astute Disraeli allow the Queen to suspect his true feelings about Balmoral. His appreciation was expressed with customary fulsomeness. 'He seemed delighted with his stay and was most grateful,' she noted after his first visit. 'He certainly seems more concerned for my comfort than any preceding Prime Minister . . . .'

That, indeed, was the point. In his infinitely more subtle way, Disraeli succeeded where Gladstone had failed. It was due to Disraeli's adroit handling of Queen Victoria that she was finally coaxed out of her long period of mourning. By opening her eyes to the possibilities of her position, by bringing into flower her innate sense of majesty, by boosting her self-esteem, Disraeli transformed Victoria.

Under his guidance, she developed into the revered, magnificent and almost mythical figure of her old age.

We came in sight of a new country, and looked down a very fine glen – Glen Mark. We descended by a very steep but winding path, called The ladder, very grand and wild.'

* * *

In 1883 one of Queen Victoria's strongest links with Scotland was severed: John Brown died, aged 56 years, of erysipelas – a condition worsened by a chill and by the chronic alcoholism of his later years. The court was at Windsor at the time and the Queen, on her own admission, was 'utterly crushed'. Her life, she admitted to her secretary, 'has again sustained one of those shocks', like in 1861 when, on the death of Prince Albert, 'every link has been shaken and torn'.

For six days Brown's body lay in state at Windsor and then the coffin, adorned with the Queen's wreath, travelled north for burial in Scotland. When it was finally laid to rest in Crathie cemetery, near Balmoral, the pall covering the coffin was the tartan plaid which had always accompanied the Queen and her gillie on their many outings in the Highlands.

Just as Queen Victoria had previously directed her energies to the immortalization of her late husband, so did she now set about preserving the memory of her Highland gillie. No less a poet than Tennyson was commanded to compose the lines inscribed on the headstone of Aberdeen granite that marked Brown's grave; to these lines the Queen added an even more heartfelt inscription in which the gillie was referred to as 'the beloved friend of Queen Victoria'. The sculptor Edgar Boehm created a life-sized bronze statue which was set up outside one of the Queen's little retreats on the Balmoral estate so that, in death as in life, Brown could keep guard over his mistress as she sat in the open air, working at her State papers.

In less than a year after Brown's death, Queen Victoria published a second instalment of her account of life at Balmoral – *More Leaves from the Journal of a Life in the Highlands*. As before, these simple memoirs found great favour with the general public and caused considerable embarrassment in the Queen's circle. Most embarrassing of all was the frequency with which Brown's name cropped up. Not only did it appear on almost every page and in a specially added 'Conclusion' but the book was dedicated, in the most effusive terms, to his memory.

As if this were not bad enough, the Queen then announced her intention of writing 'a little memoir' of her faithful gillie. In it, she planned to prove that he had been 'a great deal more' than just a devoted servant.

This is what her entourage was afraid of. Indeed, the finished manuscript caused consternation in her household. One by one, various eminent men, having read her 'little memoir', advised against the making of 'such intimate and most sacred feelings' public. They could so easily be misunderstood by 'less sensitive' readers. But the Queen held firm. Only when the Dean of Windsor plucked up the courage to tackle her on the subject did she change her mind. The Queen might have been obstinate but she would never have been so foolish as to ignore the advice of those who had nothing but her interests at heart.

But if ever evidence were needed of the innocence of the Queen's relationship with her Highland gillie, it is provided by the eagerness with which she was prepared to tell the world about it.

*   *   *

A feature of Queen Victoria's life at Balmoral, which was to become almost legendary, was the daily drive. Come wind, rain or sleet, the Queen would never miss it. 'I remember a morning when none of the family would accompany Grandmama Victoria in her little pony carriage,' recalled Princess Alice, afterwards Countess of Athlone, 'so, to my intense joy and pride, I was deputed and out we went, sleet pouring down on us, nothing daunted.'

Eugénie, the widowed ex-Empress of the French, would often be the Queen's guest at Birkhall, on the Balmoral estate; and the Empress's young friend, the composer Ethel Smyth, has left an even more vivid description of the Queen's imperviousness to the weather.

A storm of such violence was raging on the day that the Queen was due to drive over to Birkhall from Balmoral to visit the Empress that Ethel Smyth imagined that no one, especially no old lady, would ever venture out in it. She was wrong. Not only did the Queen arrive, but she arrived in an open carriage unprotected by any rugs or wraps. Her Majesty never caught cold. 'Some of her ladies,' noted Miss Smyth, 'were old and frail, but the rigours of a Scotch "waiting", including a north-east wind *with rain*, were evidently nullified by the glow of loyalty within their bosoms. On the other hand, dread of displeasing "the dear Queen" may have had something to do with it.'

The Queen arrived punctually at 3 o'clock. Throughout the entire visit she made not the slightest reference to the tempest raging outside. Only when a gillie came banging on the drawing-room door, to tell her that she would have to go as the horses could stand it no longer, did she rise to leave. Even though John Brown was dead by now, Victoria allowed herself to be spoken to by her gillies in a fashion that would have earned anyone else a very sharp rebuke.

'We got out at the chapel [at Rosslyn], which is in excellent preservation; it was built in the fifteenth century, and the architecture is exceedingly rich. . . . Twenty Barons of Rosslyn are buried there in armour.'

'On the bridge [over the Linn of Dee] Lady Fife received us, and we all drank in whisky "prosperity to the bridge." The view of the linn is very fine from it.'

The rain, which had been falling all afternoon, now began to pour down with even more vehemence. It was coming down, says Ethel Smyth, like a continuous waterfall. Raising her voice above the noise of the storm, she asked one of Victoria's ladies whether the Queen would have the carriage closed going home. By leaning well towards her, Ethel was just able to catch what she calls her serene reply. 'Oh dear no,' said the lady-in-waiting. 'I think not.' And as Ethel watched the departure from behind one of the firmly closed windows of the house, she saw that this 'incredible prediction' was fulfilled.

With back erect and head held high, the plump little figure of the Queen of England was borne away in an open barouche through the blinding cascade of October rain.

*   *   *

Perhaps the most exotic figure ever to form part of Queen Victoria's Balmoral entourage was the man who, to a certain extent, replaced John Brown in her affections: an Indian by the name of Abdul Karim.

Karim had joined the Queen's service, as a waiter, in 1887 – the year of her Golden Jubilee – and had quickly made himself all but indispensable to her. Given the title of 'The Queen's Indian

Memorial cross to
H.R.H. the Princess Alice.

Secretary', he was more usually referred to as 'the Munshi', or teacher, because one of his duties was to teach the Queen Hindustani. A handsome man who rapidly ran to fat, the Munshi appears to have been deceitful, pompous and self-seeking, with none of John Brown's honest-to-goodness qualities. But the Queen would not hear a word against him. In her eyes, and in the face of all evidence to the contrary, the Munshi could do no wrong.

At Balmoral the Munshi lived in the specially built Karim Cottage. Surrounded by a 20-foot palisade, the house accommodated not only the Munshi but his wife and various other relations. A more bizarre ménage set down amidst the wilds of upper Deeside, could hardly be imagined. The Munshi, on the Queen's orders, always wore clothes 'styled in the Indian fashion' with white or gold turbans. His wife, noted Victoria, was 'beautifully dressed with green and red and blue gauzes, spangled with gold', while her mother wore 'tight-fitting silk and satin trousers, topped by a knee-length tunic'.

Life within this self-contained compound was lived along strict Muhammadan lines; animals were slaughtered according to religious rites. It all seemed, wrote one of the Queen's ladies-in-waiting, 'so un-English, so essentially Oriental'. It was certainly very un-Scottish.

Throughout the dozen or so years that the Munshi spent in Victoria's service (he was with her until she died) his presence was hotly resented by her household. They found his arrogance insufferable. There were numberless rows. One of the most serious of these occurred at Balmoral in 1897 when *The Graphic* published a large photograph captioned 'The Queen's Life in the Highlands: Her Majesty receiving a lesson in Hindustani from the Munshi Hafiz Abdul Karim C. I. E.' In it the diminutive old Queen is seen sitting at a table signing documents. Towering over her, plump and imperious, stands the Munshi. Of the important position he held in the Queen's entourage, and esteem, there could be no doubt.

The publication of the photograph infuriated the household. They were more infuriated still when they discovered that it was the Munshi who had ordered the photographer to have the picture published in *The Graphic*. But their fury was as nothing when compared to that of the Munshi himself. He bitterly resented the fact that the household had discussed the matter with the photographer, and he took his resentment out on the Queen. The poor Queen, by now very much dominated by the Munshi, was greatly upset. She had come to dread his harangues.

Yet it never occurred to her to get rid of him. For the Munshi fulfilled a very necessary role in the Queen's life. Surrounded by so much deference and gentility, she may well have welcomed someone who would speak back to her. This, after all, had been one of John Brown's chief attractions. What Queen Victoria had always appreciated most, not only about Brown but about the Highlanders generally, was their frankness: their way of treating her as a woman first, a queen second. And although the Munshi was far from honest, he was by now – even in his very insolence – treating her as a companion rather than as a sovereign.

* * *

At Balmoral, late in 1887, and for the first time in almost three centuries, a royal child was born in Scotland. The parents were the Queen's youngest daughter, Princess Beatrice, and her husband, Prince Henry of Battenberg. The infant, christened in the Balmoral drawing-room, should have been given, as her fourth name, the old Gaelic name of Eua but the Dean of the Order of the Thistle, imagining the name to have been mis-spelled, baptized her as Ena. The infant, always known as Ena, grew up to marry King Alfonso XIII and to become the Queen of Spain.

Prince and Princess Henry of Battenberg having, on the Queen's insistence, made their home with her, were by now a permanent feature of her life at Balmoral. The ebullient Prince Henry did much to brighten the Queen's days. Indeed, life at Balmoral was far livelier during the last decade of the nineteenth century than at any time since Prince Albert's death. Not only the four Battenberg children but a selection of the Queen's other grandchildren would often be in the house. To these would be added members of the dynasty staying in nearby houses: the Prince of Wales's family at Abergeldie, others at Birkhall.

But Victoria did not need to rely solely on her ever-expanding family for diversion and entertainment. There would be amateur theatricals performed by members of the household. The D'Oyly Carte Company presented *The Mikado*; actors of the calibre of the Bancrofts, Beerbohm Tree and Forbes Robinson all performed at Balmoral. Visitors would be welcomed by torchlight processions, reels would be danced in front of the castle and nothing would induce the Queen to miss the annual Gillies' Ball. In fact, she had resumed dancing herself.

'After dinner,' she noted one evening in 1890, 'the other ladies and gentlemen joined us in the Drawing Room and we pushed the furniture back and had a nice little impromptu dance, Curtis's band being so *entraînant*.' She danced a quadrille with her Wales grandson, Prince Albert Victor; 'then followed some waltzes and polkas'.

The following year when, at the age of 72, the Queen danced with Prince Henry of Battenberg, her astonished secretary reported that she danced 'light airy steps in the old courtly fashion; no limp or stick but every figure carefully and prettily danced'.

In 1895 she attended the opening and dedication of the new Crathie church. Some of the money for the project had been raised by the holding of a huge bazaar at which members of the royal family manned the stalls to sell their own handiwork. The Queen is said to have given a wry smile on being told that not all her basketwork had been sold.

Regular visitors, such as the Empress Eugénie, would be augmented by more exotic guests: the handsome and immensely rich Rao of Kutch, or the Queen of Romania who, under the pseudonym of Carmen Sylva, wrote plays and poetry. Far and away the most important visitors were Tsar Nicholas II and the Empress Alexandra of Russia, who came in the autumn of 1896. The Empress was yet another of that great tribe of the Queen's grand-daughters – Princess Alicky of Hesse. The visiting Russians, accustomed to the sybaritic warmth and luxury of their palaces, found upper Deeside – even in September – almost unbearably cold. To this was added wind, rain and – as far as the Tsar was concerned – dismal sport. But the old Queen was delighted to be entertaining them; 'It seems quite like a dream having dear Alicky and Nicky here'.

The dream was captured for posterity when, on the last day of the visit, the company was photographed by what the Queen called 'the new cinematograph process – which makes moving pictures by winding off a reel of films'. To this day one can see that moment in history on the terrace at Balmoral: a jerky representation of the Queen walking, the Queen being led in her pony chair, the royal children skipping about, the imperial couple selfconsciously strolling. On seeing the film, Queen Victoria pronounced it 'a very wonderful process'.

Inevitably, as Queen Victoria approached her eightieth birthday, her health began to fail. Her energy drained away, her appetite worsened, her eyesight weakened, rheumatism kept her from sleeping. At the same time, personal and political troubles seemed to crowd in. There were the deaths of many of those close to her, including her son Prince Alfred and her son-in-law Prince

Henry of Battenberg. She was distressed by the outbreak of the Boer War in 1899.

'Again my old birthday returns, my eighty-first!' she wrote at Balmoral on 24 May 1900. 'God has been merciful and supported me, but my trials and anxieties have been manifold, and I feel tired and upset by all I have gone through this winter and spring.'

She returned to Scotland, for the last time, that autumn. At the end of her stay, she was driven, as usual, around the Balmoral estate to take her leave of the various cottagers. To one of the aproned women who came out, wiping her hands, to greet her, the Queen said, 'I have come to say goodbye to you, and I hope you will have a comfortable winter, and keep well till I come back.'

But she did not come back. Within three months she was dead. Queen Victoria's 60-year-long association with 'the proudest, finest country in the world' – the country in which she had spent the happiest days of her long life – was over.

'Independently of the beautiful scenery, there was a quiet, a retirement, a wilderness, a liberty, and a solitude that had such a charm for us.'

Overleaf: Glen Lyon

Wildness and Art

· 1 ·

The Border Country

QUEEN Victoria's passion was for the wild rugged grandeur of the Scottish Highlands. Consequently, like so many others similarly afflicted with this love, she tended to overlook the gentler pastoral charm of the Borders until quite late on in her life. This prejudice is perhaps a little surprising, considering her affection for the words of Sir Walter Scott. As she both quoted several extracts from his novels and poems in her *Journals*, and visited associated locations, it is not unreasonable to imagine that she might have sought out that landscape which dominates much of Scott's work earlier in her travels through Scotland. However, on her visit to the Border region, she did visit his home at Abbotsford and mentions relevant locations, such as in her recollections of Melrose Abbey.

Even today the Abbey ruins are magnificent, which is quite remarkable considering the ravagings which the original building received during the regular cross-border skirmishes which occurred for several centuries after its founding by King David I in 1136. (Though this is perhaps due in no small part to the financial attention given to it by the Duke of Buccleuch and Sir Walter Scott.) My personal interest in such edifices lies in the arches and roofs, which always provide creative material for photography; and they were no disappointment. The Abbey, however, is also

The Eildon Hills.

intriguing for its stonework: it possesses some of the oldest carvings in Scotland, in a myriad different colours and shades, which provide interesting close-ups.

The Abbey is overshadowed by the Eildon Hills, which also dominate the landscape for some miles. The Queen recalls that there was originally one hill reputedly split into three by the wizard, Michael Scott. In fact, the legend of the hills relates merely that he set the task for the Devil in the hope of keeping him eternally occupied. Unfortunately this provided only one night's endeavour for the Prince of Darkness, but the legend also records that Scott finally succeeded in his goal by setting him the awesomely endless undertaking of spinning ropes from sea sand.

On the side of one of the hills can be seen the Eildon Tree Stone, where Thomas the Rhymer met and fell in love with the Queen of the Faeries. Besotted, he followed her into the mountain to Faeryland where he remained for seven blissful years; he later committed an account of his sojourn to verse.

Melrose Abbey.

Perhaps even more impressive than the ruins of Melrose Abbey are those of Tantallon Castle, perched precariously on a cliff edge on the east coast. The castle's almost impregnable position helps to account for its strategic importance, and only rarely did the garrison capitulate to invaders. Even its capture by the all-conquering Cromwellian army under General Monk required a continuous bombardment of 12 days. Sadly the natural erosion of the sea has ensured that there is less of the fortifications to view than was seen by Queen Victoria and, indeed, today it is in such imminent danger of collapse that it will be necessary to artificially strengthen and protect the foundations. Whilst the castle itself is well worth a visit, the real pleasure, one shared by Queen Victoria, is taking a picnic on the nearby cliffs with their fine view of the Forth Estuary and the dominating Bass Rock. Though now only host to a lighthouse and thousands of screeching seabirds, the rock has in its time been a religious hermitage to St Baldred, a prison to hold convenanting ministers, and a fortress. In its latter role, it was even more successful than the nearby castle, on one occasion being held for three years by a group of Jacobite officers.

Visit to Floors and the Scotch Border Country 1867

Thursday, August 22.

. . . Then we drove up to *St. Boswell's Green*, with the three fine *Eildon* hills before us – which are said to have been divided by

Michael Scott, the wizard – seeing *Mertoun*, my excellent Lord Polwarth's place, on the other side of the road. Alas! he died only last Friday from a second stroke, the first of which seized him in February; and now, when he had intended to be at the head of the volunteers who received me at *Kelso*, he is lying dead at his house which we passed so near! It lies low, and quite in among the trees. I lament him deeply and sincerely, having liked him very much, as did my dearest Albert also, ever since we knew him in 1858.

We changed horses at *Ravenswood*, or old *Melrose* (where I had my own), having caught a glimpse of where *Dryburgh Abbey* is, though the railway almost hides it. The Duke of Buccleuch met us there, and rode the whole way. Everywhere, wherever there were dwellings, there was the kindest welcome, and triumphal arches were erected. We went by the side of the *Eildon Hills*, past an immense railway

Melrose Abbey.

The Bass Rock in the Forth Estuary.

viaduct, and nothing could be prettier than the road. The position of *Melrose* is most picturesque, surrounded by woods and hills. The little village, or rather town, of *Newstead*, which we passed through just before coming to *Melrose*, is very narrow and steep. We drove straight up to the *Abbey* through the grounds of the Duke of Buccleuch's agent, and got out and walked about the ruins, which are indeed very fine, and some of the architecture and carving in beautiful preservation. David I, who is described as a 'sair Saint', originally built it, but the Abbey, the ruins of which are now standing, was built in the fifteenth century. We saw where, under the high altar, Robert Bruce's heart is supposed to be buried; also the tomb of Alexander II, and of the celebrated wizard, Michael Scott. Reference is made to the former in some lines of Sir Walter Scott's in the 'Lay of the Last Minstrel', which describes this Border country :-

> They sat them down on a marble stone;
> A Scottish monarch slept below.

And then when Deloraine takes the book from the dead wizard's hand, it says –

> He thought, as he took it, the dead man frowned.

Most truly does Walter Scott say –

> If thou wouldst view fair Melrose aright,
> Go visit it by the pale moonlight.

It looks very ghostlike, and reminds me a little of *Holyrood Chapel*. We walked in the churchyard to look at the exterior of the Abbey, and then re-entered our carriages and drove through the densely crowded streets.

Visit to Broxmouth.

Monday, August 26 [1878].

. . . another turn or two brought us to *Tantallon*, which is close to and overhangs the sea. We drove along the grass to the old ruins, which are very extensive. Sir Hew Dalrymple, to whom it belongs, received us, and took us over the old remains of the moat, including the old gateway, on which the royal standard had been hoisted. Lady Dalrymple (a Miss Arkwright) received us. No one else was there but Sir David Baird, who had joined us on the way on horseback. Sir Hew Dalrymple showed me about the ruins of this very ancient castle, the stronghold of the Douglases. It belonged once to the Earl of Angus, second husband to Queen Margaret (wife of James IV), and was finally taken by the Covenanters.

It was unfortunately so hazy that we could not distinguish the *Bass Rock*, though usually it is quite distinctly seen, being so near; and all the fine surrounding coast was quite invisible. There was a telescope, but we could see nothing through it; it was, besides, placed too low. Seated on sofas near the ledge of the rock, we had some tea, and the scene was extremely wild.

Tantallon Castle.

· 2 ·

Inveraray

DURING her stay in Inveraray, Queen Victoria made several excursions around the shores of Loch Dhub. On more than one occasion, short relaxed trips were made up Glen Shira, past the loch, which bears the same name as one of her favourite places near Balmoral. As she herself points out, that is the only similarity between the two, for this one is bounded by much gentler rolling hills; a far more pastoral subject for her palette. Glen Shira never really becomes the typical rugged Scottish glen, even at its head where stand the ruins of Rob Roy's house. As such, I would imagine it has always been relatively accessible, so one wonders why the legendary bandit chose here to hide out, rather than one of the many other far more remote places.

The excursion up through Ardkinglas, over into Glen Croe and down to the shores of Loch Lomond, passes through two glens which are much more typical of the kind of terrain tourists expect. In the recent past, technological innovations have enabled a new road to be built, but even well into the age of the motorized vehicle, the main thoroughfare followed the route of the original military road built by Caulfield between 1746 and 1748. Though this tarmac passage is now prohibited to vehicles, much of it still remains intact and so provides an excellent pedestrian route. Along Glen Kinglas, the long straight leads to the head of the glen, turning right through deserted crofts up onto the flat summit of the pass, in which nestles Loch Restel. I personally love this loch and often stop here on journeys, because its situation, surrounded by peaks, means that more often than not it presents itself half in light and half in shadow, thus making a dramatic photographic subject. However, the most exhilarating part of the road comes soon after this. The road twists in a series of very severe S-bends down into Glen Croe and proceeds along the bottom beneath the jagged sheer walls of Beinn Ime and Ben Arthur (the Cobbler). To experience the true impressiveness of the engineering feat which provided the original military road, it is best to walk this section in reverse. Aching limbs and bursting lungs will also explain the very apt name given to the high point of the road by pre-mechanized travellers: 'Rest and Be Thankful'.

Visit to Inveraray, September 1875.

Wednesday, September 22.

... then came upon the shore of *Loch Fyne*, the drive along which is lovely. As we drove, the setting sun bathed the hills in crimson, – they had been golden just before, – the effect was exquisite. Looking up and down the shores, the view was lovely, and the reflections on the calm surface of the lake most beautiful. ...

Thursday, September 23.

... You come rapidly upon the *Dhu Loch*, a small but very pretty loch – a complete contrast to our *Dhu Loch*, for this is surrounded by green and very wooded hills, with the extremely pretty and picturesque *Glen Shira* in the background, which is richly wooded. ...

Tuesday, September 28.

... At a quarter to four started off in a shower in the waggonnette, with Louise, Beatrice, and Jane Churchill, for *Glen Shira*. We drove by the approach through the fine old avenue of beeches which suffered so much two years ago. This time along the right side of the *Dhu Loch*, which is three-quarters of a mile long, up to the head of *Glen Shira*, which is seven miles distant from the head of the loch, and is lovely. We had driven up a good way last Thursday as far as *Drumlee*. It is a lovely glen, wilder and much shut in as you advance, with fine rocks appearing through the grassy hills, and thickly wooded at the bottom. We passed two farms, and then went up to where the glen closes, and on the brae there is a keeper's cottage, just above which are the remains of a house where Rob Roy lived for some time concealed, but on sufferance. His army or followers were hidden in *Glen Shira*.

Loch Fyne.

We got out here to look at some fine falls of the river *Shira*, a linn falling from a height to which footpaths had been made. Then drove on a little farther, and stopped for tea. We stopped twice afterwards to make a slight sketch of this lovely green glen, so picturesque and peaceful-looking, and then to take another view from the lower end of the *Dhu Loch*, in which Louise helped me. . . .

Wednesday, September 29.

. . . We passed *Ardkinglass* (Mr. Callander's), and then turned up to the left through the very wild and desolate *Glenkinglass*. The high green hills with hardly any habitations reminded me of the *Spital of Glenshee*. The mist lifted just enough to let one see the tops of the hills below which we were passing. The road was steep, and, just as we were getting near the top, the leaders, which had repeatedly stopped, refused to pull any farther, reared and kicked and jibbed, so that we really thought we should never get on, and should perhaps have to sleep at some wayside inn. But we stopped, and Brown had the leaders taken off near a small tarn, called *Loch Restel*, and he

Portrait of H.R.H. the Princess Beatrice.

*Dubh Loch
in Glen Shira.*

Adkinglas.

Loch Restel.

and Francie walked. We then got on much better. A little farther on we passed a few scattered huts, and at last we reached the top of this long ascent. The rain, which had been very heavy just when our plight was at its worst, stopped, and the day cleared.

At the summit of the pass is the spot called *Rest and be thankful*, from an inscription cut upon a stone by the regiment that made the road, which was one of the military roads to open up the *Highlands* constructed by Government under the superintendence of Marshal Wade. The stone still remains, but the words are much defaced. Here we came upon the splendid steep wild pass of *Glen Croe*, something like *Glencoe*, but not so fine and the road much steeper. It reminds me of the *Devil's Elbow*, and even of the *Devil's Bridge* in the *Göschenen Pass* on the *St. Gothard*. We got out and walked down the road, which goes in a zigzag. A few people who had walked up from the coach were standing there. As at *Glencoe* the stream flows in the hollow of the pass, and there were some cattle and a house or two. The sun even came out all at once and lit up the wild grand scene. We got into the carriage near the bottom, and drank Fritz and Vicky's healths.

'Rest and Be Thankful'.

· 3 ·

The Invertrossachs

QUEEN Victoria made an extensive boating trip along the whole length of Loch Lomond, though she wasn't the first monarch to make such an excursion. The previous one, however, was not so kindly disposed towards the natives, nor of British origin; in reaching the loch to carry out his pillage and suchlike during 1263, King Haakon IV of Norway actually had to drag his longships overland from the sea. In travelling rather more sedately across the water, the Queen provides a commentary of which today's pleasure-cruiser captains would be proud.

This whole area of the Trossachs is now one of the major tourist areas of Scotland, and is consequently very busy, especially at weekends when numbers are swelled by day-excursions from Glasgow. As far as Loch Lomond is concerned, the historical interests as documented by the Queen have obviously contributed to its popularity, but a major watersports complex at the aptly named Duck Bay, the use of Luss as the location for the filming of the Scottish soap *Take the High Road* and the growth of mountain-walking have also contributed to its extensive commercialization.

In my opinion the last three factors have all in some way damaged the character of the area. I am particularly saddened by the case of Ben Lomond, because the relatively easy access to the summit, and close proximity to densely populated urban areas, means that many of those who tramp on it are not dedicated genuine hill-walkers and do not appear to have much consideration for the environment. Consequently the mass excursions up this mountain's slopes have created seriously eroded tracks which now resemble six-lane motorways, and the summit doubles as a council refuse-tip. This mountain is not alone in having suffered this despoliation, a similar fate having befallen Ben Nevis and parts of Cairngorm, but it is perhaps the most seriously affected.

Queen Victoria's deep affection for the Highlands, quite apart from the scenery, was born out of the quiet solitude which the wilderness afforded her. In retracing her routes, I wondered what her impression of the land would be if she were making her expeditions today, when much of the aspect which so charmed her has been lost forever amongst the throngs of tourists.

There are, however, within the Highlands, still some areas relatively untouched by the hand of wanton commercialism. Unfortunately they are not around the Trossachs and, probably equal with Loch Lomond as the most debauched locations of natural beauty, is its near neighbour of Loch Katrine. Poor Sir Walter Scott might probably have spared the place and not used it as the setting for his most famous poem, 'The Lady of the Lake', had he foreseen the outcome of his actions. Though the popularity of his work has generally declined in recent years, this particular poem and the associated landscape alone have retained, through Scott's words, the same universal appeal and magic for visitors today as they did for Queen Victoria. However, even for her, and the already considerable influx of literarily-aware travellers of the time, a most important landmark of the ballad had been already forever removed from searching eyes. For when the loch was designated to provide water for the population of Glasgow, and when the 34-mile underwater aqueduct to facilitate this was built, the water-mark had to be raised to a point where it covered the Silver Strand.

From an illustrative point of view, I have always found the area a very difficult subject to portray professionally, because it is very hard to obtain a perspective which other cameras have not already captured, or a scene devoid of human elements. This problem is enhanced by the heavy hand of the metropolitan chiefs who threaten all manner of dire consequences to any souls straying from the concrete promenade and who, by the use of boards, themselves wreak greater havoc with the loch's beauty than those who they intend to dissuade could ever do.

The other entry for this area which I have chosen from Queen Victoria's *Journals* is again one which was instigated by her appreciation of Scott's prose. This expedition culminates at the graveyard of Balquhidder where lies the subject of Scott's 'Rob Roy'. The life exploits of the clan chief, which were such an inspiration for the author, were actually far less romantic than those of the hero of the novel: whilst the real MacGregor was something of a legend for his resistance to the English, he was also a common brigand who was not above committing acts of murder and theft against his fellow countrymen.

Though a mere handful of miles from the crowded centres of the Trossachs, the church, the Braes of Balquhidder and Loch Voil still form a peaceful landscape where one can meander in comparative solitude. This is even more true now, since the recently improved highway inspires such high-speed driving that many people miss the turn-off onto the minor road leading to this natural paradise. This insane desire to press the accelerator pedal through the floor of the car may be a reaction to the difficulties of negotiating the earlier section of road around the shore of Loch Lubnaig. The twisting road may be somewhat hair-raising for the driver but the enforced slow progress will at least allow the passengers, not otherwise engaged in dodging

Loch Lomond.

oncoming traffic on the wrong side of the road or preventing a catastrophic plunge into the water, to appreciate the loch's grandeur in much the same leisurely way as Queen Victoria. It is an unusual, almost L-shaped loch which reminded the Queen of parts of Switzerland. One location on its shore, just before the water begin the descent through the Pass of Leny, is the ruined Chapel of St Bride. Genealogically-minded transatlantic visitors would probably be interested to learn that this is the resting place of six generations of ancestors of US President McKinley.

Visit to Invertrossachs, 1869.

Saturday, September 4.

. . . We went at once on board the fine steamer 'Prince Consort' (a pleasant idea that that dear name should have carried his poor little wife, alas! a widow , and children, on their first sail on this beautiful lake which he went to see in 1847). She is a fine large vessel, a good deal larger than the 'Winkelried' (in which we used to go on the *Lake of Lucerne*), with a fine large dining-cabin below, a very high upper deck, and a gallery underneath on which people can stand and smoke without incommoding the others above. The following people were on board: Mr. A. Smollett, late M.P., Mr. Wylie, factor to Sir T. Colquhoun, and Mr. Denny, the auditor, and Mr. Young, the secretary.

We steamed southward, and for the first half nothing could be finer or more truly Alpine, reminding me much of the *Lake of Lucerne*; only it is longer – *Loch Lomond* being twenty-two miles long. We kept close to the east shore, passing under *Ben Lomond* with its variously called shoulders – *Cruachan, Craig a Bochan*, and *Ptarmigan* – to *Rowardennan* pier, where there is a pretty little house rented from the Duke of Montrose (to whom half *Loch Lomond* belongs) by a Mr. Mair, a lovely spot from whence you can ascend *Ben Lomond*, which is 3,192 feet high, and well wooded part of the way, with cornfields below. After you pass this, where there are fine mountains on either side, though on the west shore not so high, the lake widens out, but the shores become much flatter and tamer (indeed to the east and south completely so); but here are all the beautifully wooded islands, to the number of twenty-four. Some of them are large, on *Inchlonaig Island* the yews are said to have been planted by Robert Bruce to encourage the people in the use of archery. Another, *Inch Cailliach*, is the ancient burial place of the MacGregors.

Loch Lomond and Ben Lomond.

On the mainland we passed *Cornick Hill*, and could just see *Buchanan House*, the Duke of Montrose's, and to the right the island of *Inch Murrin*, on which the Duke has his deer preserve. The sun had come out soon after we went on board, and it was blowing quite fresh as we went against the wind. At two o'clock we stopped off *Portnellan* for luncheon, which we had brought with us and took below in the handsome large cabin, where fifty or sixty people, if not more, could easily dine. Colonel Ponsonby also lunched with us. . . . This over, we went to the end of the lake to *Balloch*, and here turned. It became very warm. To the left we passed some very pretty villas (castles they resembled) and places, amongst others *Cameron* (Mr. Smollett's), *Arden* (Sir J. Lumsden's, Lord Provost of Glasgow), *Ross-Dhu* (Sir J. Colquhoun's), the road to *Glen Fruin*, the islands of *Inch Conachan, Inch Tavanach*, the point of *Stob Gobhlach, Luss*, a very prettily situated village, the mountain of *Ben Dubh*, and the ferry of *Inveruglas*, opposite *Rowardennan*. Then *Tarbet*, a small town, where dearest Albert landed in 1847, and here began the highest and finest mountains, with splendid passes, richly wooded, and the highest mountains rising behind. A glen leads across from *Tarbet* to *Arrochar* on *Loch Long*, and here you see that most singularly shaped hill called the *Cobbler*, and a little further on the splendid *Alps of Arrochar*. All this and the way in which the hills run into the lake reminded me so much of the *Nasen* on the *Lake of Lucerne*.

The head of the lake with the very fine glen (*Glen Falloch*), along which you can drive to *Oban*, is magnificent. We (Louise and I) sketched as best we could, but it is most difficult to do so when the steamer keeps moving on; and we were afterwards much vexed we had not asked them to go more slowly, as we had to wait again for the 'Rob Roy' steamer at *Stronachlachlar*. From the head of *Loch Lomond* (where is the *Hotel of Inverarnan*) we turned; we were shown a hole in the rock, on the east side, which they called *Rob Roy's Cave*, and landed at *Inversnaid*. The people (quite a small crowd) threw bunches of heather as we passed. Heather is everywhere the decoration, and there is indeed no lovelier, prettier ornament. It was in such full bloom. The mountains here are peculiarly fine from the sharp serrated outline and wonderful clothing of grass and trees. . . .

Thursday, September 2.

. . . It was about ten minutes past five when we went on board the very clean little steamer 'Rob Roy' – the very same we had been on under such different circumstances in 1859 on the 14th of October, in dreadful weather, thick mist and heavy rain, when my beloved Husband and I opened the *Glasgow Waterworks*. We saw the spot and the cottage where we lunched.

H.R.H. the Princess Louise.

Loch Katrine.

We took a turn and steamed a little way up the bay called *Glen Gyle*, where there is a splendid glen beautifully wooded, which is the country of the MacGregors, and where there is a house which belonged to MacGregor of *Glen Gyle*, which, with the property, has been bought by a rich Glasgow innkeeper of the same clan. We turned and went on, and nothing could be more beautiful than the loch, wooded all along the banks. The rugged *Ben Venue*, so famed in the 'Lady of the Lake' (which we had with us as well as several guide-books, of which we find Black's far the best), rises majestically on the southern side of the lake, and looking back you see the *Alps of Arrochar*, which well deserve the name, for they are quite pointed and most beautiful; their names are *Ben Vean*, *Ben Voirlich*, *Ben Eim*, and *Ben Crosh*. Next came the well-known 'Silver Strand', 'Helen's Isle', which is most lovely, and the narrow creek so beautifully wooded below the splendid high hills, and the little wooden landing-place which I remembered so well; and very melancholy and yet sweet were my feelings when I landed and found on the path some of the same white pebbles which my dearest Albert picked up and had made into a bracelet for me. I picked up and carried off a handful myself.

We had taken our tea on board on deck. We now entered two hired carriages, the girls and I in the first, with Brown on the box, and Jane Churchill and Colonel Ponsonby in the second. The evening was lovely, and the lights and pink and golden sky as we drove through the beautiful *Trossachs* were glorious indeed –

> So wondrous wild, the whole might seem
> The scenery of a fairy dream –

and along *Loch Achray* – the setting sun behind *Ben Venue*, which rose above most gloriously, so beautifully described by Sir W. Scott:

> The western waves of ebbing day
> Rolled o'er the glen the level way.
> Each purple peak, each flinty spire
> Was bathed in floods of living fire. . . .

Friday, September 3.

. . . We went along the truly beautiful *Loch Lubnaig*, driving along its windings like the *Axenstrasse* on the *Lake of Lucerne*, the high, jagged, and green hills rising precipitously from it. It is four miles long, and very romantic. There is a railway unfinished, only a single line, on the western side, and as it ran along the loch it again reminded me of the *Axenstrasse* at the points where it goes low near the water. The road leads under beautiful sycamore trees. We passed on the right a farmhouse called *Ardhullary*, where formerly the Abyssinian traveller Bruce used to live, and next entered *Strathyre*, a fine broad open strath, wooded and with cornfields, the heather on the hills quite pink. The village of *Strathyre* is composed of a row of a few peasants' houses, with very poor people, and a nice well-built little inn. A little way on again you come to a picturesque little inn called the *King's House*, covered with pretty creepers and convolvulus, and here you turn short to the left and go up *Balquhidder*, another most lovely glen, with a beautiful view of *Loch Voil* with its beautiful sweeping green hills, the *Braes of Balquhidder*, the strath itself very rich with its fine trees and cornfields, the small river *Balvaig* running through it. We drove about two miles, passing some pretty cottages covered in creepers like the inn I mentioned and stopped outside a neat-looking little village, the *Kirkton of Balquhidder* (twelve miles from *Callander*), composed of only a few cottages. We got out and walked up a steep knoll over-hanging the road, on which, under a splendid plane tree (we passed some most beautiful limes just before), is the old kirk-yard with the ruins of the old church. We went at once to look at the tomb of Rob Roy – a flat stone on which is carved the figure in a kilt, and next to it a stone where his wife is buried, and on which a sword is rudely carved.*

His son's tomb is next to his, but looks far more modern. We went on to look at a very curious old font, and then at two or three other tombstones. On one of these were some verses, which Mr. Cameron, the schoolmaster, an intelligent young man, recited, and afterwards wrote out for me.

The words of the inscription are:–

ISABEL CAMBELL,
SPOUSE TO MR ROBERT KIRK, MINISTER,
DIED 25 DECEMBER, 1680.
SHE HAD TWO SONS, COLIN AND WILLIAM.
HER AGE 25.

Stones weep tho' eyes were dry;
Choicest flowers soonest die:
Their sun oft sets at noon,
Whose fruit is ripe in June.
Then tears of joy be thine,
Since earth must soon resign
To God what is divine.

Nasci est aegrotare, vivere est sæpe mori, et mori est vivere.

LOVE AND LIVE.

We afterwards went into the very pretty new church, which is close to the old ruin. Nothing can surpass the beauty of the position of this spot, for it overlooks *Loch Voil* and a glen, or rather mere ravine or corry, with a hill rising behind it.

* These stones are supposed to be very ancient, and carved centuries before they are adapted to their present use.

Loch Lubnaig.

Loch Achray and Ben Venue.

Loch Voil.

· 4 ·

Tayside

QUEEN Victoria's first encounter with Loch Tay was during her initial excursion to Scotland. She was taken by rowing boat almost the full length of it and, being her first experience of the real Highlands, the impact it obviously made was instrumental in forging the beginnings of her life-long affair with the country. From the boat, the vastness of Ben Lawers must have seemed awesome, even though – as time went on – she would view, and indeed climb, far more dramatic examples of rock. On neither this visit nor a subsequent one did she express any desire to view the loch from this higher vantage point, thereby missing a panorama I am sure she would have greatly appreciated. Now, the easiest route to the summit of Ben Lawers, as on its sisters Lomond and Nevis, entails walking through a sad landscape of human destruction. In this case, however, the ravaging of the slopes has been almost artificially hastened and encouraged by the very organization which complains about the erosive capabilities of armies of Vibram-soled trekkers.

Perhaps the natural trickle of dedicated scramblers would never have multiplied into the regularly ascending army if this self-same organization had not built a commercialized visitor's centre with attached car-park half way up the poor Ben's back! As here, the changes in Glen Dochart would seem tremendous to

Victoria if she were alive today and able to compare it with her early travel, for it is now dissected by a straight tarmac highway designed to transport the tourist as rapidly as possible from one cash-guzzling venue to another.

By contrast, the route between Loch Tay and Killiecrankie via Glen Lyon, apart from at some stage having had tarmac laid over the original byway, is probably still the same as it was on the occasion of the royal passage, except in part of Glen Lyon where it now follows the opposite bank of the river. Even here, however, the old road is visible, and so are some of the bridges which Queen Victoria very probably walked across. Passing through Fortingall, it is hard to imagine that this village is reputed to be the birthplace of a man whose subsequent actions took on great religious significance and created perhaps the most important festival in the Christian calendar. It was here that a Roman ambassador to northern Britain is said to have taken a wife, from either the Clan Menzies or the Clan MacLaren of Balquhidder, who presented him with a son – Pontius Pilate.

From high on the 'dreary' moor, Schiehallion does not look particularly spectacular; neither is it a very difficult climb to the summit. However, this Fairy Mountain of the Caledonians, which has such a distinctive outline if viewed from other peaks, has a very special place in scientific history: in 1774, experiments to determine the weight of the earth were conducted on its summit. One of the investigating team, a mathematician named Charles Hutton, also used the opportunity to develop research which eventually resulted in his invention of contour lines. So perhaps I, like many other walkers, owe a debt to this mountain for the many times when I have been thankful to use those map-lines in order to leave a ridge or summit by the safest descent.

The entry for October 3, 1866, is the only one in the *Journals*, where I would respectfully question the Queen's otherwise impeccably factual text. As she rightly points out, on her previous visit she never went to the place which she imagines was affectionately named after her as 'The Queen's View'. Whilst the view which presents itself from this location is worthy of such a title, the likelihood is that the royal reference is to the visit by Mary in 1564, when she too was enraptured by the landscape to such an extent that she commanded her harpist to praise it in music.

First Visit to Scotland.

Saturday, September 10 [1842].

... With us were Lord Breadalbane and the Duchess of

Norfolk and Duchess of Buccleuch; and two pipers sat on the
bow and played very often. I have since been reading in
The Lady of the Lake, and this passage reminds me of our
voyage :–

> See the proud pipers on the bow,
> And mark the gaudy streamers flow
> From their loud chanters, and sweep
> The furrow'd bosom of the deep,
> As, rushing through the lake amain,
> They plied the ancient Highland strain.

Our row of 16 miles up *Loch Tay* to *Auchmore*, a cottage of
Lord Breadalbane's, near the end of the lake, was the prettiest
thing imaginable. We saw the splendid scenery to such great
advantage on both sides: *Ben Lawers*, with small waterfalls
descending its sides, amid other high mountains wooded here
and there; with *Kenmore* in the distance; the view, looking
back, as the loch winds, was most beautiful. The boatmen
sang two Gaelic boat-songs, very wild and singular; the
language so guttural and yet so soft. Captain McDougall, who
steered, and who is the head of the McDougalls, showed us the
real 'brooch of Lorn', which was taken by his ancestor from
Robert Bruce in a battle. The situation of *Auchmore* is exquisite; the trees growing so beautifully down from the top of the
mountains, quite into the water, and the mountains all round,
make it an enchanting spot. We landed and lunched in the
cottage, which is a very nice little place. The day was very fine;
the Highlanders were there again. We left *Auchmore* at twenty
minutes past three, having arrived there at a quarter before
three. The kindness and attention to us of Lord and of Lady
Breadalbane (who is very delicate) were unbounded. We
passed *Killin*, where there is a mountain stream running over
large stones, and forming waterfalls.

The country we came to now was very wild, beginning at
Glen Dochart, through which the *Dochart* flows; nothing but
moors and very high rocky mountains, We came to a small
lake called, I think, *Laragilly*, amidst the wildest and finest
scenery we had yet seen. *Glen Ogle*, which is a sort of long
pass, putting one in mind of the prints of the *Kyber Pass*, the
road going for some way down hill and up hill, through these
very high mountains, and the escort in front looking like mere
specks from the great height. We also saw *Ben Voirlich*. At
Loch Earn Head we changed horses. Lord Breadalbane rode

Loch Tay.

Glen Dochart.

with us the whole way up to this point, and then he put his Factor (in Highland dress) up behind our carriage. It came on to rain, and rained almost the whole of the rest of the time. We passed along *Loch Earn*, which is a very beautiful long lake skirted by high mountains; but is not so long or so large as *Loch Tay*. Just as we turned and went by St Fillans, the view of the lake was very fine. There is a large detached rock with rich verdure on it, which is very striking.

Second Visit to Dunkeld.

Wednesday, October 3, [1866].

. . . Immediately after this we came upon the bridge, and *Loch Tay*, with its wooded banks, clear and yet misty, burst into view. This again reminded me of the past – of the row up the loch, which is sixteen miles long, in 1842, in several boats, with pibrochs playing, and the boatmen singing wild Gaelic songs. The McDougall steered us then, and showed us the real Brooch of Lorne taken from Robert Bruce.

To the right we could see the grounds and fine park, looking rather like an English one. We stopped at *Murray's Lodge*, but, instead of changing horses here, drove five miles up the loch, which was quite clear, and the stillness so great that the reflection on the lake's bosom was as strong as though it were a real landscape. Here we stopped, and got out and sat down on the shore of the loch, which is covered with fine quartz, of which we picked up some; took our luncheon about half-past one, and then sketched. By this time the mist had given way to the sun, and the lake, with its richly wooded banks and changing foliage, looked beautiful.

At half-past two we re-entered our carriage, the horses having been changed, and drove back up a steep hill, crossing the river *Lyon* and going into *Glenlyon*, a beautiful wild glen with high green hills and rocks and trees, which I remember quite well driving through in 1842 – then also on a misty day: the mist hung over, and even in some places below the tops of the hills. We passed several small places – *Glenlyon House*, the property of F.G. Campbell of *Troup*. To the left also *Fortingal* village – Sir Robert Menzies' – and a new place called *Dun-aven House*. Small, picturesque, and very fair cottages were dotted about, and there were others in small clusters; beautiful sycamores and other trees were to be seen near the river-side. We then passed the village of *Coshieville*, and turned by the hill-road – up a very steep hill with a burn flowing at the

bottom, much wooded, reminding me of *M'Inroy's Burn* –
passed the ruins of the old castle of the Stewarts of *Garth*, and
then came on a dreary wild moor – passing below *Schiehallion*, one of the high hills – and at the summit of the road came
to a small loch, called *Ceannairdiche*.

Soon after this we turned down the hill again into woods,
and came to *Tummel Bridge*, where we changed horses. Here
were a few, but very few people, who I think, from what Brown
and Grant – who, as usual, were in attendance – said, recog-
nised us, but behaved extremely well, and did not come near.
This was at twenty minutes to four. We then turned as it were
homewards, but had to make a good long circuit, and drove
along the side of *Loch Tummel*, high above the loch, through
birch wood, which grows along the hills much the same as
about *Birkhall*. It is only three miles long. Here it was again

Loch Tay.

very clear and bright. At the end of the loch, on a highish point called after me '*The Queen's View*' – though I had not been there in 1844 – we got out and took tea. But this was a long and unsuccessful business; the fire would not burn, and the kettle would not boil. At length Brown ran off to a cottage and returned after some little while with a can full of hot water, but it was no longer boiling when it arrived, and the tea was not good. Then all had to be packed, and it made us very late.

It was fast growing dark. We passed *Alleine*, Sir Robert Colquhoun's place, almost immediately after this, and then, at about half-past six, changed horses at the *Bridge of Garry*, near, or rather in the midst of, the *Pass of Killiecrankie*; but from the lateness of the hour and the dullness of the evening – for it was raining – we could see hardly anything.

Killiekrankie.

The wild moors on Schiehallion overlooking Lochan on Daim.

· 5 ·

Tayside East

IN 1844, when staying at Blair Castle, the Queen made several excursions up Glen Tilt, and thence onto several of the ridges and summits in the vicinity. She also attended a deer drive at this location, which seems to have been a popular place for such royal activities: other previous royal observers included James V in 1529 and Mary, Queen of Scots in 1564. The glen itself actually provides a right of way for some 22 miles through to the Linn of Dee, a route which the Queen also used in 1861. This makes an excellent walk, but the glen is also a superb location for less active visitors, thanks mainly to the Atholl estates. These estates, for a small fee, allow vehicles to drive as far as Forest Lodge, after which the glen narrows to a rocky gorge which is impassable to all but walkers anyway. Thus, a very beautiful region can be explored by parking the car and either making short excursions up the slopes or just ambling along the river banks. Even on the latter there are many small waterfalls and interesting colourful rock formations to discover. For example, near the aptly named Marble Lodge, there are the remains of workings from which, in the last century, marble was taken for use in Edinburgh.

Within close proximity to the glen, and still on the Atholl estates, are the Falls of Bruar, made famous by the words of Burns' 'Petition' which lamented the lack of afforestation. The well laid out and maintained pathways here provide excellent circular tours with not only spectacular views of the various falls but also beautiful meandering walks through the forest approaches.

This was my first visit to Dunkeld. Previously, when travelling on the A9, I had bypassed it, being bound for more northerly destinations. But it is definitely worth visiting, and I can understand why Queen Victoria made more than one excursion here. The town, with Scone, was once the joint capital of Scottish lands when Kenneth McAlpine united the Scots and Picts in AD 844. The Cathedral at Dunkeld has rather a sad history: though it was begun in 1318, it was not actually completed until 1501 and then, merely 60 years later, it was reduced to a roofless ruin. Its exquisite location on the banks of the Tay is overlooked by the hill on which grew the 'walking wood' described by Shakespeare; the Birnam Wood which came to high Dunsinane and signalled the end of Macbeth.

A few miles east of the town is the Loch of the Lowes, which though a very beautiful stretch of water, seems to have missed the attention afforded to other Scottish lochs because it has the misfortune not to be surrounded by rugged peaks. However, its pleasant shores are now becoming more popular because of its growing reputation as an excellent nature reserve. The part of the Queen's text which fascinated me was the reference to the Rumbling Bridge a few miles to the west along the Braan River. I wasn't disappointed because, as I approached, there was indeed a rumble or, as I could put it, more of a mighty roar; when you stand on the bridge, the vibrations caused by the cascading water can be felt right through the stonework. It is a unique experience which I have encountered on no other bridge, and one which is quite unnerving because, even though the bridge has withstood the phenomenon for some time, I was in constant fear that the foundations might shake themselves apart. It also posed an intriguing problem: the water falls in a fast-moving torrent over a long drop to a rocky pool under the bridge, but when it reappears from the other side it is a relatively slow-moving current. The pool must be tremendously deep to be able to absorb the energy and reduce the flow to such an extent.

First Visit to Dunkeld.

Wednesday, October 11 [1865].

. . . After this we drove round the three *Lochs* of the *Lowes*–viz.

The Loch of the Lowes.

Dunkeld Cathedral.

The Rumbling Bridge.

Craig Lush, Butterstone, and the *Loch of the Lowes* itself (which is the largest). They are surrounded by trees and woods, of which there is no end, and are very pretty. We came back by the *Blairgowrie* road and drove through *Dunkeld* (the people had been so discreet and quiet, I said I would do this), crossing over the bridge (where twenty-two years ago we were met by twenty of the Athole Highlanders, who conducted us to the entrance of the grounds), and proceeded by the upper road to the *Rumbling Bridge*, which is Sir William Stewart of *Grandtully's* property. We got out here and walked to the bridge, under which the *Braan* flowed over the rocks most splendidly; and, swollen by the rain, it came down in an immense volume of water with a deafening noise. Returning thence we drove through the village of *Inver* to the *Hermitage* on the banks of the *Braan*, which is *Dunkeld* property. This is a little house full of looking-glasses, with painted walls, looking on another fall of the *Braan*, where we took tea almost in the dark. It was built by James, the second Duke of Athole, in the last century. . . .

Thursday, October 12 [1865].

A fair day, with no rain, but, alas! no sunshine. Brown's leg was much better, and the doctor thought he could walk over the hill to-morrow.

Excellent breakfasts, such splendid cream and butter! The Duchess has a very good cook, a Scotchwoman, and I thought how dear Albert would have liked it all. He always said things tasted better in smaller houses. There were several Scottish dishes, two soups, and the celebrated 'haggis', which I tried last night, and really liked very much. The Duchess was delighted at my taking it.

At a quarter past twelve Lenchen and I walked with the Duchess in the grounds and saw the Cathedral, part of which is converted into a parish church, and the other part is a most picturesque ruin. We saw the tomb of the Wolf of Badenoch, son of King Robert the Second. There are also other monuments, but in a very dilapidated state. The burying-ground is inside and south of the Cathedral. We walked along the side of the river *Tay*, into which the river *Braan* flows, under very fine trees, as far as the American garden, and then round by the terrace overlooking the park, on which the tents were pitched at the time of the great déjeuner that the Duke, then Lord Glenlyon, gave us in 1842, which was our first acquaintance with the *Highlands* and Highland customs; and it was such a fine sight! Oh! and here we were together – both widows!

* * *

Visit to Blair Athole.

Thursday, September 12 [1844].

. . . At a little before four o'clock Albert drove me out in the pony phaeton till nearly six—such a drive! Really to be able to sit in one's pony carriage, and to see such wild, beautiful scenery as we did, the farthest point being only five miles from the house, is an immense delight. We drove along *Glen Tilt*, through a wood over-hanging the river *Tilt*, which joins the *Garry*, and as we left the wood we came upon such a lovely view, – *Beny-y-Ghlo* straight before us – and under these high hill the river *Tilt* gushing and winding over stones and slates, and the hills and mountains skirted at the bottom with beautiful trees; the whole lit up by the sun; and the air so pure and fine; but no description can at all do it justice, or give the idea what this drive was.

Oh! what can equal the beauties of nature! What enjoyment there is in them! Albert enjoys it so much; he is in ecstasies here. He has inherited this love of nature from his dear father. . . .

Saturday, September 21 [1844].

After breakfast Albert saw Lord Glenlyon, who proposed that he should go deer-stalking and that I should follow him. At twenty minutes to eleven we drove off with Lady Canning for *Glen Tilt*. The day was glorious and it would have been a pity to lose it, but it was a long hard day's work, though extremely delightful and enjoyable, and unlike anything I had ever done before. I should have enjoyed it still more had I been able to be with Albert the whole time.

We drove nearly to Peter Fraser's house, which is between the *Marble Lodge* and *Forest Lodge*. Here Albert and I walked about a little, and then Lady Canning and we mounted our ponies and set off on our journey, Lord Glenlyon leading my pony the whole way, Peter Fraser, the head-keeper (a wonderfully active man) leading the way; Sandy and six other Highlanders carrying rifles and leading dogs, and the rear brought

Above Bruar Falls.

Glen Tilt rocks.

Bruar Falls.

up by two ponies with our luncheon-box. Lawley,* Albert's Jäger, was also there, carrying one of Albert's rifles; the other Albert slung over his right shoulder, to relieve Lawley. So we set off and wound round and round the hill, which had the most picturesque effect imaginable. Such a splendid view all round, finer and more extensive the higher we went! The day was delightful; but the sun very hot. We saw the highest point of *Ben-y-Ghlo*, which one cannot see from below, and the distant range of hills we had seen from *Tulloch* was beautifully softened by the slightest haze. We saw *Loch Vach*. The road was very good, and as we ascended we had to speak in a whisper, as indeed we did almost all day, for fear of coming upon deer unawares. The wind was, however, right, which is everything here for the deer. I wish we could have had Landseer with us to sketch our party, with the background, it was so pretty, as were also the various 'halts,' &c. If I only had had time to sketch them!

We stopped at the top of the *Chrianan*, whence you look down an immense height. It is here that the eagles sometimes sit. Albert got off and looked about in great admiration, and walked on a little, and then remounted his pony. We then went nearly to the top of *Cairn Chlamain*, and here we separated, Albert going off with Peter, Lawley, and two other keepers, to get a 'quiet shot' as they call it; and Lady Canning, Lord Glenlyon, and I went up quite to the top, which is deep in moss. Here we sat down and stayed some time sketching the ponies below; Lord Glenylon and Sandy remaining near us. The view was quite beautiful, nothing but mountains all around us, and the solitude, the complete solitude, very impressive. We saw the range of *Mar Forest*, and the inner range to the left, receding from us, as we sat facing the hill, called *Scarsach*, where the counties of *Perth*, *Aberdeen*, and *Inverness* join. My pony was brought up for me, and we then descended this highest pinnacle, and proceeded on a level to meet Albert, whom I descried coming towards us. Wet met him shortly after; he had had bad luck, I am sorry to say. We then sat down on the grass and had some luncheon; then I walked a little with Albert and we got on our ponies. As we went on towards home some deer were seen in *Glen Chroime*, which is called the 'Sanctum'; where it is supposed that there are a great many. Albert went off soon after this, and we remained on *Sron a*

* A very good man. His health obliged him to give up being a Jäger in 1848; he was then appointed a Page, in which position he continued till he died, in November, 1865.

Chro, for an hour. I am sure, as Lord Glenlyon said by so doing we should turn the deer to Albert, whereas if we went on we should disturb and spoil the whole thing. So we submitted. Albert looked like a little speck creeping about on an opposite hill. We saw four herds of deer, two of them close to us. It was a beautiful sight.

Meanwhile I saw the sun sinking gradually, and I got quite alarmed lest we should be benighted, and we called anxiously for Sandy, who had gone away for a moment, to give a signal to come back. We then began our descent, 'squinting' the hill, the ponies going as safely and securely as possible. As the sun went down the scenery became more and more beautiful, the sky crimson, golden-red and blue, and the hills looking purple and lilac, most exquisite, till at length it set, and the hues grew softer in the sky and the outlines of the hills sharper. I never saw anything so fine. It soon, however, grew very dark.

At length Albert met us, and he told me he had waited all the time for us, as he knew how anxious I should be. He had been very unlucky, and had lost his sport, for the rifle would not go off just when he could have shot some fine harts; yet he was as merry and cheerful as if nothing had happened to disappoint him. We got down quite safely to the bridge; our ponies going most surely, though it was quite dusk when we were at the bottom of the hill. We walked to the *Marble Lodge*, and then got into the pony carriage and drove home by very bright moonlight, which made everything look very lovely; but the road made one a little nervous. . . .

Monday, September 16 [1844].

. . . Albert drove me (Lord Glenlyon riding with us) to the *Falls of Bruar*. We got out at the road, and walked to the upper falls, and down again by the path on the opposite side. It is a walk of three miles round, and a very steep ascent; at every turn the view of the rushing falls is extremely fine, and looking back on the hills, which were so clear and so beautifully lit up, with the rapid stream below, was most exquisite. We threw stones down to see the effect in the water. The trees which surround the falls were planted by the late Duke of Athole in compliance with Burn's '*Petition*'.

The evening was beautiful, and we feasted our eyes on the ever-changing, splendid views of the hills and vales as we drove back. Albert said that the chief beauty of mountain scenery consisted in its frequent changes.

· 6 ·

The Mounth

BALMORAL is surrounded by mountains which are often incorrectly grouped together and referred to as The Grampians. In fact, to the north of the Dee river are the Cairngorms (which are similarly misnamed) and to the south, The Mounth. Taking into account Queen Victoria's naturally adventurous spirit and zest for exploration, it is not surprising that she made ascents to many of the summits. These 'Great Expeditions' as she called them were always in the company of Prince Albert and, after his death, though using some of the high roads across the plateaux to travel, her desire to attain the highest peaks was never rekindled.

Her first ascent was Lochnagar, which as it dominates the royal estate, is quite understandable. Being the first, and considering the conditions she described, it would have been no surprise if she had abandoned the attempt and decided that this mode of exploration was unbecoming for a monarch. The fact that she didn't is a clear indication of her fearless determination. Sadly, my bravery fell far short of Her Majesty's when I began the ascent in similar conditions. High on its slopes, I was carefully plodding through the swirling cloak of mist when it thinned briefly enough for me just to discern the outline of the sheer precipices over which I could easily blunder. So, as once again a blinding thick blanket obscured all beyond the tip of my nose, I decided that, not

Glen Callater.

wishing the photographs to be published posthumously, I would retreat.

The granite slopes of the mountain had already attained a permanent prominence in British literature when Byron, on his journey through Scotland, had climbed the peak and been so impressed by its grandeur that he immortalized it in verse.

> England! thy beauties are tame and domestic
> To one who has roved o'er the mountains afar:
> Oh, for the Crags that are wild and majestic!
> The steep frowning glories of dark Loch na Gar.

I wonder if he, like Queen Victoria, is referring to the mountain because this is, in fact, the wrong term for it. The name 'Lochnagar' is a corruption of 'Lochan na Gaire' meaning the tarn of noisy sound', which strictly speaking describes the water deep in the corrie. Over a period of time this name has been transferred to the collection of peaks which form this corrie; the correct term for the plateau is the White Mounth and each of the peaks has an individual title. In the case of two of these, Cac Carn Beag and Cac Carn Mór, the names embarrassingly translate as 'Little Shit Cairn' and 'Big Shit Cairn' respectively, which probably explains why the collective name was given.

The Queen's expedition through Glen Callater over the Monega road to the precipitous picnic area overhanging Caenlochan was a happy one at the time but ultimately must have provided a very sad memory for the Queen; it proved to be the last Great Expedition, with the death of Prince Albert intervening between this and her subsequent visit to Balmoral. A good deal of the land she covered on the second half of this particular journey is now frequented by skiers using the Glenshee slopes.

Last Expedition.

Wednesday, October 16, 1861.

. . . Near *Castleton*, and indeed all along the road, in the shade, the frost still lay, and the air was very sharp. We took posthorses at *Castleton*, and proceeded up *Glen Clunie* to *Glen Callater*, which looked lovely, and which Albert admired much. In a little more than two hours we were at *Loch Callater* – the road was very bad indeed as we approached the loch, where our ponies were waiting for us. After walking a few paces we remounted them, I on my good 'Fyvie', and Alice on 'Inchrory'.

The day was glorious – and the whole expedition delightful, and very easily performed. We ascended *Little Cairn Turc*, on the north side of *Loch Callater*, up a sort of footpath very easy and even, upon ground that was almost flat, rising very gradually, but imperceptibly; and the view became wonderfully extensive. The top of *Cairn Turc* is quite flat – with moss and grass – so that you could drive upon it. It is very high, for you see the high table-land behind the highest point of *Loch-na-Gar*. On that side you have no view; but from the other it is wonderfully extensive. It was so clear and bright, and so still there, reminding us of the day on *Ben Muich Dhui* last year.

There rose immediately behind us *Ben Muich Dhui*, which you hardly ever see, and the shape of which is not fine, with its surrounding mountains of *Cairngorm, Brae Riach, Ben Avon* or *A'an, Ben-na-Bhourd*, etc. We saw *Ben-y-Ghlo* quite clearly, and all that range of hills; then, further west, *Schichallion*, near *Loch Tay*; the mountains which are near the *Black*

Loch Callater.

Carn an Tuirc.

The slopes of Lochnagar.

Lochnagar.

Mount; and, quite on the horizon, we could discern *Ben Nevis*, which is above *Fort William*.

Going up *Cairn Turc* we looked down upon *Loch Canter*, a small loch above *Loch Callater*, very wild and dark. We proceeded to *Cairn Glashie*, at the extreme point of which a cairn has been erected. We got off to take a look at the wonderful panorama which lay stretched out before us. We looked on *Fifeshire*, and the country between *Perth* and *Stirling*, the *Lomond Hills*, etc. It was beautifully clear, and really it was most interesting to look over such an immense extent of the *Highlands* . . .

We walked on a little way, and then I got upon my pony. Another half hour's riding again over such singular flat table-land, brought us on to the edge of the valley of *Cairn Lochan*, which is indeed 'a bonnie place'. It reminded me and Louise of *Clova*; only there one did not see the immense extent of mountains behind. *Cairn Lochan* is a narrow valley, the river *Isla* winding through it like a silver ribbon, with trees at the bottom. The hills are green and steep, but towards the head of the valley there are fine precipices. We had then to take a somewhat circuitous route in order to avoid some bogs, and to come to a spot where we looked right up the valley for an immense distance; to the left, or rather more to the south, was *Glen Isla*, another glen, but wider, and not with the same high mountains as *Cairn Lochan*. Beyond *Glen Isla* were seen the *Lomond Hills* behind *Kinross*, at the foot of which is *Loch Leven*.

We sat on a very precipitous place, which made one dread any one moving backwards; and here, at a little before two o'clock, we lunched. The lights were charmingly soft, and, as I said before, like the bloom on a plum. The luncheon was very acceptable, for the air was extremely keen, and we found ice thicker than a shilling on the top of *Cairn Turc*, which did not melt when Brown took it and kept it in his hand.

Helena was delighted for this was *the only really great* expedition in which she had accompanied us.

Duncan and the keeper at *Loch Callater* (R. Stewart) went with us as guides.

I made some hasty sketches; and then Albert wrote on a bit of paper that we had lunched here, put it into the Selters-water bottle, and buried it there, or rather stuck it into the ground. Grant had done the same when we visited *Ben Muich Dhui* the first time. This over, we walked part of the way back which we had ridden to avoid the bogs – we ladies walking

H.R.H. the Princess Helena.

only a short way, and then riding. We altered our course, and left *Cairn Glashie* to our right, and went in the direction of the *Cairn Wall*. Looking back on the distant hills above *Glen Isla* and *Cairn Lochan* (Lord Airlie's 'Country'), it was even more beautiful; for, as the day advanced, the mountains became clearer and clearer, of a lovely blue, while the valleys were in shadow. *Shichallion*, and those further ranges, were also most perfectly to be seen, and gave me much a longing for further Highland expeditions!

First Ascent of Loch-na-Gar.

Saturday, September 16, 1848.

. . . Albert saw some deer when we had been out about three-quarters of an hour, and ran off to stalk them, while I rested; but he arrived just a minute too late. He waited for me on the other side of a stony little burn, which I crossed on my pony, after our faithful Highlanders had moved some stones and made it easier. We then went on a little way, and I got off and walked a bit, and afterwards remounted; Macdonald leading my pony. The view of *Ben-na-Bhourd*, and indeed of all around, was very beautiful; but as we rose higher we saw mist over *Loch-na-Gar*. Albert left me to go after ptarmigan, and went on with Grant, while the others remained with me, taking the greatest care of me. Macdonald is a good honest man, and was indefatigable, and poor Batterbury was very anxious also.

I saw ptarmigan get up, and Albert fire – he then disappeared from my sight, and I rode on. It became cold and misty when we were on *Loch-na-Gar*. In half an hour, or rather less, Albert rejoined me with two ptarmigan, having come up by a shorter way. Here it was quite soft, easy walking, and we looked down on two small lochs called *Na Nian*, which were very striking, being so high up in the hills. Albert was tired, and remounted his pony; I had also been walking a little way. The ascent commenced, and with it a very thick fog, and when we had nearly reached the top of *Loch-na-Gar*, the mist drifted in thick clouds so as to hide everything not within one hundred yards of us. Near the peak (the fine point of the mountain which is seen so well from above Grant's house) we got off and walked, and climbed up some steep stones, to a place where we found a seat in a little nook, and had some luncheon. It was just two o'clock, so we had taken four hours going up.

· 7 ·

Loch Muick

QUEEN Victoria spent much of her time around this loch during her sojourns at Balmoral Castle. She regularly visited Loch Muick, staying at the secluded Alt-na-Giuthasach on the shore, where she spent many intimate loving days with Albert. Not surprisingly, after the Prince Consort's death, she could not bear to live in the house and she had another shiel built, much further along the loch where the Glas-allt burn flows into it.

Considering her reasons for the change of venue, this choice of location was a little strange; it was after all, at the very place where Albert, throughout his life, had expressed a desire to build a lodge. During her period of mourning, which was to last throughout her life, the loch took on a new significance. As she now moved alone amidst the rugged grandeur which both she and Albert had loved together, she was constantly reminded of the deep loving companionship which she had lost. In this way, the loch perhaps caused a conflict of emotions because, while its presence provided memories of the many happy times, it also seemed to compound her deep sense of loss. It is quite ironic that the English translation of the name Loch Muick is 'The Lake of Sorrow'. The Queen pointed this out early in her *Journals*, though obviously without the knowledge of just how poignantly relative it would become for her.

Dubh Loch is also very aptly named, though more with regard to its features. It is indeed a 'Black Lake' upon which the sun rarely shines, being blocked out for much of the year by the north-east rock-face, rising sheer from the water's edge. This cliff, in addition to being one of the highest in the British Isles, is not only visually stunning, but also provides some extremely testing routes for climbers. Though the other enclosures are not quite so severe, when approaching through the narrow easy defile, the atmosphere is still quite claustrophobic and more than a little sinister. Regardless of this, or perhaps even because of it, the loch was a favourite haunt of Queen Victoria and her family.

It was during an excursion here, via the Falls of Glas-allt, which cascade spectacularly into Loch Muick, that the Queen recalls being given the sad news of the death of the Duke of Wellington. I have chosen this passage from her last *Journal* to contrast with the elation which she felt on her first visit to the area. With the sombreness of these words influencing my photographic intentions, I set forth in atrocious conditions, which I hoped might help recreate the atmosphere of melancholic lamentation, to illustrate this passage. When it rains in the Highlands, it does so with a vengeance, and so it did on this day. As the lens was uncovered, it became smeared with water which, when wiped away, was resmeared faster than my hand could travel from cloth to shutter- release. This consequently provided me with a very effective, if somewhat inconsistent, natural soft focus, for which I will thank Mother Nature, and a long delicate equipment-drying session, for which I will not.

View of the Glas-allt Shiel.

CLASSALT SHIEL.

The First Stay at Alt-na-Giuthasach.

August 30, 1849.

... We lunched as soon as we arrived, and at three walked down (about twenty minutes' walk) to the loch called 'Muich'; which some say means 'darkness' or 'sorrow'. Here we found a large boat, into which we all got, and Macdonald, Duncan, Grant, and Coutts rowed; old John Gordon and two others going in another boat with the net. They rowed up to the head of the loch, to where the *Muich* runs down out of the *Dhu Loch*, which is on the other side.

The scenery is beautiful here, so wild and grand,–real severe Highland scenery, with trees in the hollow. We had various scrambles in and out of the boat and along the shore, and saw three hawks, and caught seventy trout. I wish an artist could have been there to sketch the scene: it was so picturesque – the boat, the net, and the people in their kilts in the water, and on the shore. ...

Loch Muich.

September 16, 1850.

... They rowed mostly towards the opposite side, which is very fine indeed, and deeply furrowed by the torrents, which form glens and corries where birch and alder trees grow close to the water's edge. We landed on a sandy spot below a fine glen, through which flows the *Black Burn.* It was very dry here; but still very picturesque, with alder-trees and mountain-ash in full fruit overhanging it. We afterwards landed at our usual place at the head of the loch, which is magnificent; and rode back. A new road has been made, and an excellent one it is, winding along above the lake.

The moon rose, and was beautifully reflected on the lake, which, with its steep green hills, looked lovely. To add to the beauty, poetry, and wildness of the scene, Cotes played in the boat; the men, who row very quickly and well now, giving an occasional shout when he played a reel. It reminded me of Sir Walter Scott's lines in *The Lady of the Lake:-*

> 'Ever, as on they bore, more loud
> And louder rung the pibroch proud.
> At first the sound, by distance tame,
> Mellow'd along the waters came,
> And, lingering long by cape and bay,
> Wail'd every harsher note away.

Visit to the Dhu Loch, etc.

September 11, 1849.

. . . It was half-past twelve when we began ascending the hill immediately behind the house, and proceeded along over the hills, to a great height, whence the view was very fine, quite overhanging the loch, and commanding an extensive view of *Glen Muich* beyond on the opposite side. The road got worse and worse. It was particularly bad when we had to pass the *Burn of the Glassalt*, which falls into the loch, and was very full. There had been so much rain, that the burns and rivers were very full, and the ground quite soft. We rode over the *Strone Hill*, the wind blowing dreadfully hard when we came to the top. Albert walked almost from the first, and shot a hare and a grouse; he put up a good many of them. We walked to a little hollow immediately above the *Dhu Loch*, and at half-past three seated ourselves there, and had some very welcome luncheon. The loch is only a mile in length, and very wild; the hills, which are very rocky and precipitous, rising perpendicular from it.

In about half an hour we began our journey homewards. We came straight down beside the *Muich*, which falls in the most beautiful way over the rocks and stones in the glen. We rode down, and only had to get off to cross the *Glassalt*, which was an awkward ford to scramble over. The road was rough, but certainly far less soft and disagreeable than the one we came by.

Account of the News of the Duke of Wellington's Death.

Alt-na-Giuthasach, Thursday, September 16, 1852.

. . . We walked on until we reached the higher part of the *Glassalt*, which we stepped across. We had passed over the tops of these hills on that expedition to the *Dhu Loch* three years ago, when the ground was so soft, that ponies could scarcely get along, the roads were so very bad.

Then we began the descent of the *Glassalt*, along which another path has been admirably made. From here it is quite beautiful, so wild and grand. The falls are equal to those of the *Bruar* at *Blair*, and are 150 feet in height; the whole height to the foot of the loch being 500 feet. It looked very picturesque to see the ponies and Highlanders winding along. We came down to the *Shiel of the Glassalt*, lately built, where there is a charming room for us, commanding a most lovely view. Here

Loch Muick.

Rocks in Glas-allt.

Loch Muick.

we took the cold luncheon, which we had brought with us; and after that we mounted our ponies, and rode to the *Dhu Loch*, along a beautiful path which keeps well above the burn, that rushes along over flat great slabs of stone. The scenery is exquisite. We passed a small fall called the *Burn of the Spullan* ('spout'). In half or three quarters of an hour we were at the wild and picturesque *Dhu Loch*.

We got off our ponies, and I had just sat down to sketch, when Mackenzie returned, saying my watch was safe at home, and bringing letters: amongst them was one from Lord Derby, which I tore open, and alas! it contained the confirmation of the fatal news: that England's or rather *Britain's* pride, her glory, her hero, the greatest man she ever had produced, was no more! Sad day! Great and irreparable national loss!

Glas-allt.

· 8 ·

Deeside

QUEEN Victoria spent a great deal of time in the Highlands, often as much as five months each year in the latter part of her life. The major part of these sojourns was spent, understandably, on her own property of Balmoral. Occasionally she would become the duty-bound monarch when it was required of her, as with openings and dedications such as the new Bridge at the Linn of Dee, but more usually her attendance at functions such as the Highland Games or Church thanksgivings was primarily as a member of the community and not in the role of Queen. Consequently many of the Highlanders were afforded a greater familiarity than any of her subjects in other parts of the nation. This was especially so for the estate-workers at Balmoral and their families, with whom Queen Victoria seemed to have a special relationship. Her particular concern for their welfare shows itself in her account of the drowning of the children and subsequent visit to the bereaved families. The Queen writes with such compassion and feeling that one could almost imagine it was her own kin who had lost their lives. Though today we are made aware of constant visits by members of the royal family to victims of disaster and their relatives, in Queen Victoria's time I would imagine such things were quite unheard of.

At events such as the salmon-leistering or the sheep-dipping and clipping, she was a willing observer, intrigued not only by the acts themselves but also by the workers. Her capability for diligent attention to the recording of details leaves us not only with an excellent chronicle of these events, but also with an indication that, on the remote Balmoral estate, she was perhaps at her happiest. Here she could allow her true personality to emerge and not have her emotions shackled by the restrictions necessarily imposed on one in such a position as hers.

Salmon Leistering.

September 13, 1850.

We walked with Charles, the boys, and Vicky to the river side above the bridge, where all our tenants were assembled with poles and spears, or rather 'leisters', for catching salmon. They all went into the river, walking up it, and then back again, poking about under all the stones to bring fish up to where the men stood with the net. It had a very pretty effect; about one hundred men wading through the river, some in kilts with poles and spears, all very much excited. Not succeeding the first time, we went higher up, and moved to three or four different places, but did not get any salmon; one or two escaping. Albert stood on a stone, and Colonel Gordon and Lord James Murray waded about the whole time. Duncan, in spite of all his exertions yesterday, and besides having walked to and from the Gathering, was the whole time in the water. Not far from the laundry there was another trial, and here we had a great fright. In one place there was a very deep pool into which two men very foolishly went, and one could not swim; we suddenly saw them sink, and in one moment they seemed drowning, though surrounded by people. There was a cry for help, and a general rush, including Albert, towards the spot, which frightened me so much, that I grasped Lord Carlisle's arm in great agony. However, Dr. Robertson swam in and pulled the man out, and all was safely over; but it was a horrid moment.

A salmon was speared here by one of the men; after which we walked to the ford, or quarry, where we were very successful, seven salmon being caught, some in the net, and some speared. Though Albert stood in the water some time he caught nothing: but the scene at this beautiful spot was exciting and picturesque in the extreme. I wished for Landseer's pencil. The sun was intensely hot.

Sunset over the River Dee.

Juicing the Sheep, 1868.

Thursday, October 21.

. . . This is a practice pursued all over the Highlands before the sheep are sent down to the low country for the winter. It is done to preserve the wool. Not far from the burnside, where there are a few hillocks, was a pen in which the sheep were placed, and then, just outside it, a large sort of trough filled with liquid tobacco and soap, and into this the sheep were dipped one after the other; one man (James Brown, my shepherd, the elder brother, who came up on purpose to help) took the sheep one by one out of the pen and turned them on their backs; and then William and he, holding them by their legs, dipped them well in, after which they were let into another pen into which this trough opened, and here they had to remain to dry. To the left, a little lower down, was a cauldron boiling over a fire and containing the tobacco with water and soap; this was then emptied into a tub, from which it was transferred into the trough. A very rosy-faced lassie, with a plaid over her head, was superintending this part of the work, and helped to fetch the water from the burn, while children and many collie dogs were grouped about, and several men and shepherds were helping. It was a very curious and picturesque sight.

Sheep Clipping, 1870.

Monday, June 13, 1870.

. . . all the sheep (mine) were in a pen, and James Brown, the shepherd, and Morrison, my grieve at *Invergelder*, assisted by others (one, a brother of the Morgans) took them out one by one, tied their legs together, and then placed them on the laps of the women who were seated on the ground, and who clipped them one after the other, wonderfully well, with huge scissors or clippers. Four were seated in a sort of half-circle, of whom three were Mrs. Durran, Mrs. Leys (both these did their work admirably), and Mrs. Morrison, who seemed rather new at it, and had some difficulty with these great heavy sheep, which kick a good deal. The clippers must take them between their knees, and it is very hard work. Four other women were sitting close under the wall, also clipping. Then the sheep were all marked; and some, before being clipped, had to have their horns sawn to prevent them growing into their heads. It was a very picturesque sight, and quite curious to see the splendid thick wool peel off like a regular coat.

The 'Spate', 1872.

Tuesday, June 11, 1872.

... At a little before five, set off in the waggonette with Beatrice and Janie Ely, and drove along the north side of the river. We stopped a little way beyond *Tynebaich*, and saw the people wandering along the riverside. Two women told us that two children had fallen in (how terrible!), and that one 'had been gotten – the little een' (as the people pronounce 'one'), but not the eldest. They were searching everywhere. While we were there, the old grandmother, Catenach by name, who lives at *Scutter Hole*, came running along in a great state of distress. She is Rattray's mother. We drove on a little way, and then turned round.

We heard from the people that the two boys, one of ten or eleven and the other only three, were at *Monaltrie Burn* which comes down close to the farmhouse and below Mrs. Patterson's shop, passing under a little bridge and running into the Dee. This burn is generally very low and small, but had risen to a great height – the Dee itself being tremendously high – not a stone to be seen. The little child fell in while the eldest was fishing; the other jumped in after him, trying to save his little brother; and before anyone could come out to save them (though the screams of Abercrombie's children, who were with them, were heard) they were carried away and swept by the violence of the current into the *Dee*, and carried along. Too dreadful! It seems, from what I heard coming back, that the poor mother was away from home, having gone to see her own mother who was dying, and that she purposely kept this eldest boy back from school to watch the little one.

We drove back and up to Mrs. Grant's, where we took tea, and then walked up along the riverside, and heard that nothing had been found and that the boat had gone back; but as we approached nearer to the castle we saw people on the banks and rocks with sticks searching: amongst them was the poor father – a sad and piteous sight – crying and looking so anxiously for his poor child's body. ...

Thursday, June 13.

... Brown went in first, and was received by the old grandmother, and then we went in, and on a table in the kitchen covered with a sheet, which they lifted up, lay the poor sweet innocent 'bairnie', only three years old, a fine plump child, and looking just as though it slept, with quite a pink colour, and very little scratched, in its last clothes – with its little hands joined – a most touching sight. I let Beatrice see it, and was glad she should see death for the first time in so touching and pleasing a form.

Then the poor mother came in, calm and quiet, though she cried a little at first when I took her hand and said how much I felt for her, and how dreadful it was. She checked herself, and said, with that great resignation and trust which it is so edifying to witness, and which you see so strongly here, 'We must try to bear it; we must trust to the Almighty'.

Wool.

The 'Spate'.

· 9 ·

The Cairngorms

To the north of the Dee valley are the Am Monadh Ruadh or the Red Hills, which today we know by the plural name of the best-known individual peak, Cairngorm. The range is composed of granite, a rock which weathers uniformly, thus forming the characteristic smooth-sloped bare mountains, intersected in places by equally barren glens. Within the range are found the highest peaks in Britain (apart from Ben Nevis) and several are connected by the highest plateau area. The region has long had a reputation as being the most dangerous in the British Isles. Not only is the terrain featureless, especially when coated with deep snow, but it is also very remote; many locations are as far as 12 miles away from any form of habitation, with hostile landscape in between. And if that wasn't enough the characteristics of the hills are such that the weather can change dramatically in a very short time: it is not unknown for a snow blizzard to strike the tops during June when people in Braemar or Aviemore are broiling themselves under a hot sun. There is a high incidence of walking accidents in all seasons, necessitating the launch of large-scale rescues, many of which end on a very sombre note. Consequently, whilst the whole area is spectacular and exciting, it can also be hazardous, even today with the availability of techno-logically-advanced clothing. This perhaps puts into perspective the journeys of Queen Victoria in the region where she reached the summit of several of the mountains and crossed through many of the glens; it also shows her extreme tenacity and adventurous spirit.

The excursion from Balmoral to Tomintoul takes in the far-eastern edges of the Cairngorms, via the desolate wild Loch Builg and down into the beautiful narrow valley of the Avon. This route, like most others in the area, traverses private property and, whilst pedestrians are automatically granted right of way, all routes should always be treated with due respect. After all, though it is not mandatory, the estates do greatly assist the walker by maintaining many of these paths and tracks. In no place is this more appreciated than on this route because the owner, Sir Seton Wills, has provided bridges to facilitate the crossing of the Avon. I was fortunate enough to meet this gentleman during this traverse, and I must say that his attitude to the walker on his land who wishes to enjoy its pleasures is of such a genuinely positive nature that courtesy requires reciprocal attitudes from us to his property.

I could perhaps, have, filled a whole volume with Queen Victoria's accounts of expeditions onto the heights of the Cairngorm, but space limits me to one *Journal* entry. This, with a slight detour to overlook Loch Avon with the relevant text from a different expedition, is the one which by virtue of the terrain and distance covered was the obvious one to choose. Indeed anyone who follows in these footsteps of Queen Victoria will certainly see her in a different light, especially if all their previous conceptions of her have been formed from textbook descriptions. The journey, even though assisted by pony, was completed by the royal party in one day. It is a very strenuous haul to the summit of Ben Macdui, even though much of it is along reasonable pathways. It is also one of the most visually rewarding treks I have personally ever undertaken.

A complete description is unwarranted and unnecessary, as that is more than adequately executed by the text of the *Journal*. However, if I have to mention any one aspect, apart from the exceptional panorama from the summit, it would have to be Loch Etchachan. I was stunned by the scene which unfolded as I dragged myself up the last exhausting scree to the flat basin in which the loch lies. It was, perhaps, even more breathtaking because it was under its winter mantle, but the effect on me was such that, even though the temperature was below freezing, I had to sit awhile and contemplate the beauty of the frozen waters.

The Linn of Avon.

Loch Builg.

Mr. John Grant.

Above Balmoral.

First Great Expedition:- To Glen Fishie and Grantown.

Wednesday, September 5 [1860].

... We mounted our ponies a short way out of the town, but only rode for a few minutes as it was past two o'clock. We came upon a beautiful view, looking down upon the *Avon* and up a fine glen. There we rested and took luncheon. While Brown was unpacking and arranging our things, I spoke to him and to Grant, who was helping, about not having waited on us, as they ought to have done, at dinner last night and at breakfast, as we had wished; and Brown answered, he was afraid he should not do it rightly; I replied we did not wish to have a stranger in the room, and they must do so another time.

Luncheon (provisions for which we had taken with us from home yesterday) finished, we started again, walked a little way, till we were overtaken by the men and ponies, and then rode along *Avonside*, the road winding at the bottom of the glen, which is in part tolerably wide; but narrows as it turns, and winds round towards *Inchrory*, where it is called *Glen Avon*. The hills, sloping down to the river side are beautifully green. It was very muggy – quite oppressive, and the greater part of the road deep and sloppy, till we came upon the granite formation again. In order to get on, as it was late, and we had eight miles to ride, our men – at least Brown and two of the others – walked before us at a fearful pace, so that we had to trot to keep up at all. Grant rode frequently on the deer pony; the others seemed, however, a good deal tired with the two long days' journey, and were glad to get on Albert's or the General's pony to give themselves a lift; but their willingness, readiness, cheerfulness, indefatigableness, are very admirable, and make them most delightful servants. As for Grant and Brown they are perfect – discreet, careful, intelligent, attentive, ever ready to do what is wanted; and the latter, particularly, is handy and willing to do everything and anything, and to overcome every difficulty, which makes him one of my best servants anywhere.

We passed by *Inchrory* – seeing, as we approached, two eagles towering splendidly above, and alighting on the top of the hills. From *Inchrory* we rode to *Loch Bulig*, which was beautifully lit up by the setting sun. From *Tomantoul* we escaped all real rain, having only a slight sprinkling every now and then. At *Loch Bulig* we found our carriage and four ponies, and drove back just as we left yesterday morning, reaching *Balmoral* safely at half-past seven.

Ascent of Ben Muich Dhui.

Friday, October 7, 1859.

... We rode (my pony being led by Brown most of the time both going up and down) at least four miles up *Glen Derry*, which is very fine, with the remnants of a splendid forest, *Cairn Derry* being to the right, and the *Derry Water* running below. The track was very bad and stony, and broken up by cattle coming down for the 'Tryst'. At the end of the glen we crossed a ford, passed some softish ground, and turned up to the left by a very rough, steep, but yet gradual ascent to *Corrie Etchan*, which is in a very wild rugged spot, with magnificent precipices, a high mountain to the right called *Ben Main*, while to the left was *Cairngorm of Derry*. When we reached the top of this very steep ascent (we had been rising, though almost imperceptively, from the *Derry Shiel*), we came upon a loch of the same name, which reminded us of *Loch-na-Gar* and of *Loch-na-Nian*. You look from here onto other wild hills and corries – on Ben A'an, etc. We ascended very gradually, but became so enveloped in mist that we could see nothing – hardly those just before us! Albert had walked a good deal;

Glen Derry.

Loch Avon.

and it was very cold. The mist got worse; and as we rode along the stony, but almost flat ridge of *Ben Muich Dhui*, we hardly knew whether we were on level ground or the top of the mountain. However, I and Alice rode to the very top, which we reached a few minutes past two; and here, at a cairn of stones, we lunched, in a piercing cold wind.

Just as we sat down, a gust of wind came and dispersed the mist, which had a most wonderful effect, like a dissolving view – and exhibited the grandest, wildest scenery imaginable! We sat on a ridge of the cairn to take our luncheon, – our good people being grouped with the ponies near us. Luncheon over, Albert ran off with Alice to the ridge to look at the splendid view, and sent for me to follow. I did so; but not without Grant's help, for there were quantities of large loose stones heaped up together to walk upon. The wind was fearfully high, but the view was well worth seeing. I cannot describe all, but we saw where the *Dee* rises between the mountains called the *Well of Dee – Ben-y-Ghlo* – and the adjacent mountains, *Ben*

The plateau towards Ben Macdui.

Vrackie – then *Ben-na-Bhourd* – *Ben A'an*, etc. – and such magnificent wild rocks, precipices, and corries. It had a sublime and solemn effect; so wild, so solitary – no one but ourselves and our little party there.

Albert went further on with the children, but I returned with Grant to my seat on the cairn, as I could not scramble about well. Soon after, we all began walking and looking for 'cairngorms', and found some small ones. The mist had entirely cleared away below, so that we saw all the beautiful views. *Ben Muich Dhui* is 4,297 feet high, one of the highest mountains in *Scotland*. I and Alice rode part of the way, walking wherever it was very steep. Albert and Bertie walked the whole time. I had a little whisky and water, as the people declared pure water would be too chilling.

Expedition to Loch Avon.

Saturday, September 28, 1861.

. . . We took post-horses at *Castleton*, and drove up to the *Derry* (the road up *Glen Luie* very bad indeed); and here we mounted our ponies, and proceeded the usual way up *Glen Derry*, as far as where the path turns up to *Loch Etchan*. Instead of going that way, we proceeded straight on – a dreadfully rough, stony road, though not steep, but rougher than anything we ever rode upon before, and terrible for the poor horses' feet. We passed by two little lakes called the *Dhoolochans*, opposite to where the glen runs down to *Inchrory*, and after crossing them, there was a short boggy bit, where I got off and walked some way on the opposite side, along the 'brae' of the hill, on the other side of which the loch lies, and then got on again. It was so saturated with water, that the moss and grass and everything were soaked, – not very pleasant riding, particularly as it was along the slope of the hill. We went on and on, nearly two miles from the foot of this hill, expecting to see the loch, but another low hill hid it from us, till at length we came in sight of it; and nothing could be grander and wilder – the rocks are so grand and precipitous, and the snow on *Ben Muich Dhui* had such a fine effect.

We saw the spot at the foot of *Loch Etchan* to which we scrambled last year, and looked down upon *Loch Avon*.

· 10 ·

Glen Nevis and Glen Coe

I WAS immensely delighted, upon reading the *Journals*, to learn that, whilst staying at Inverlochy, Queen Victoria took a trip along Glen Nevis, because photographically it is one of my favourite places in Scotland. From here alone, I could quite happily produce enough illustrations to fill a book. Admittedly the first mile or so does little to prepare you for the stunning scenery deeper under the shadow of Ben Nevis and its satellites, but I suppose some kind of provision must be made for campers and caravanners. However, beyond this, the real magnificence of the glen comes into its own, especially beyond the car-park at the end of the tarmac road. Below the path, the river tumbles viciously over rocky prominences; above and all around tower the peaks, forcing the glen into an ever narrower defile. Scattered about are a few hardy weather-beaten trees, and strange element-eroded stones. As it is a paradise for my lens then surely it must have been so for the Queen's paint-brushes. The one disappointment I felt regarding Queen Victoria's expeditions was that she never attempted the ascent of Ben Nevis, yet I am sure she must have seen the path at the head of this glen and, judging by her previous mountaineering exploits, I feel sure that it would have attracted her. Her interest in the summits, however, did wane considerably after the death of the Prince Consort.

On her first visit to Fort William, the Queen declined to drive through Glen Coe, though Albert went and enthused about the scenery; it was perhaps, therefore inevitable that she would take the second opportunity. The Glen Coe massacre gives the pass its reputation for being a foreboding sinister place, and it certainly lives up to this in bad conditions. When the sun is shining, however, it still manages to project an awesome atmosphere, especially if one walks the old road on which the Queen travelled. Her Majesty expressed a hope that King William was unaware of the horror perpetrated in his name. The events leading up to that fateful day, especially the change in the venue where the oath was to be taken, made by a clan chief who had already proved troublesome, was probably designed to make the outcome inevitable. Thus an example was set to the other clans of what would happen should they fail to accept the will of the English. I find it difficult to believe that the King would have no knowledge of this decision.

Victoria's perception of the landscape around her, and her ability to transpose this into words, is probably shown to no greater effect than in this *Journal* entry, though perhaps her appreciation was slightly affected by the annoyingly distracting presence of

Glen Nevis.

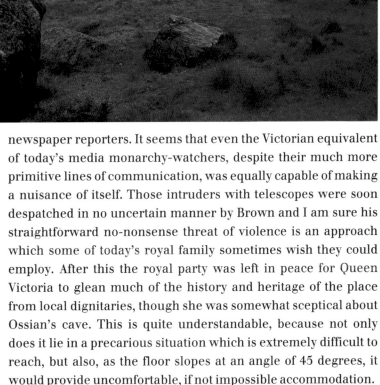

newspaper reporters. It seems that even the Victorian equivalent of today's media monarchy-watchers, despite their much more primitive lines of communication, was equally capable of making a nuisance of itself. Those intruders with telescopes were soon despatched in no uncertain manner by Brown and I am sure his straightforward no-nonsense threat of violence is an approach which some of today's royal family sometimes wish they could employ. After this the royal party was left in peace for Queen Victoria to glean much of the history and heritage of the place from local dignitaries, though she was somewhat sceptical about Ossian's cave. This is quite understandable, because not only does it lie in a precarious situation which is extremely difficult to reach, but also, as the floor slopes at an angle of 45 degrees, it would provide uncomfortable, if not impossible accommodation.

Sometimes when I read the *Journals*, or for that matter any old literary material, certain aspects or passages intrigue me, and set me thinking. Of particular interest was the silver quaich, from which a W.A. Cameron of Ballachulish offered refreshment to the Queen, which she reluctantly but politely accepted. I wonder if this vessel, which he claimed had also touched the lips of both Bonnie Prince Charlie and Prince Albert, is still in existence, if it is still in the same family and if they realize its history.

Visit to Inverlochy, 1873.

Sunday, September 14.

... At five drove out with Beatrice and Jane Churchill in the waggonette. We drove past the distillery; and then just beyond the bridge, which must be very little over two miles from *Inverlochy*, we turned off the main road. We drove up for four miles along the *Nevis*, a fine rapid burn rolling over large stones and almost forming cascades in one or two places, under fine trees with very steep green hills rising on either side, and close under and along the base of *Ben Nevis*, which rose like a giant above us. It was splendid! Straight before us the glen seemed to close; halfway up we came to a large farm, the drive to which is under an avenue of ash trees. But there is no other habitation beyond this of any kind; and soon after the trees become fewer and fewer, though still a good many grow at the burnside and up the gullies of the hills. Sheep were grazing at a great height. The road became so rough and bad that we got out and walked almost a mile, but could go no farther. We were delighted with the solemn solitude and grandeur of *Glen Nevis*; it is almost finer than *Glencoe*. There was no one when we first entered the glen, but as we walked back we met several people coming out to look. After getting into the carriage again, I stopped a little to take a rough sketch.

Saturday, September 13.

... We went on, winding under the high green hills, and entered the village of *Ballachulish*, where the slate quarries are, and which is inhabited by miners. It was very clean and tidy – a long, continuous, straggling, winding street, where the poor people, who all looked very clean, had decorated every house with flowers and bunches or wreaths of heather and

Lady Churchill, who travelled as plain Mrs. Churchill when the Queen travelled incognito.

red cloth. Emerging from the village we entered the *Pass of Glencoe*, which at the opening is beautifully green, with trees and cottages dotted about along the verdant valley. There is a farm belonging to a Mrs MacDonald, a descendant of one of the unfortunate massacred MacDonalds. The *Cona* flows along the bottom of the valley, with green 'haughs' where a few cattle are to be seen, and sheep, which graze up some of the wildest parts of this glorious glen. A sharp turn in the rough, very winding, and in some parts precipitous road, brings you to the finest, wildest, and grandest part of the pass. Stern, rugged, precipitous mountains with beautiful peaks and rocks piled high one above the other, two and three thousand feet high, tower and rise up to the heavens on either side, without any signs of habitation, except where, halfway up the pass, there are some trees, and near them heaps of stones on either side of the road, remains of what once were homes, which tell the bloody, fearful tale of woe. The place itself is one which adds to the horror of the thought that such a thing could have been conceived and committed on innocent sleeping people. How and whither could they fly? Let me hope that William III knew nothing of it.

To the right, not far on, is seen what is called *Ossian's Cave*; but it must be more than a thousand feet above the glen, and one cannot imagine how any one could live there, as they pretend that Ossian did. The violence of the torrents of snow and rain, which come pouring down, has brought quantities of stone with them, which in many parts cover the road and make it very rough. It reminds me very much of the *Devil's Bridge, St. Gothard*, and the *Goschenen Pass*, only that is higher but not so wild. When we came to the top, which is about ten miles from *Ballachulish*, we stopped and got out, and we three sat down under a low wall, just below the road, where we had a splendid view of those peculiarly fine wild-looking peaks, which I sketched.

Their Gaelic names are *Na tri Peathraichean* (*the Three Sisters*), but in English they are often called '*Faith, Hope*, and *Charity*'.

We sat down on the grass (we three) on our plaids, and had our luncheon, served by Brown and Francie, and then I sketched. The day was most beautiful and calm. Here, however – here, in this complete solitude, we were spied upon by impudently inquisitive reporters, who followed us everywhere; but one in particular (who writes for some of the Scotch papers) lay down and watched with a telescope and

*The Three Sisters,
Glen Coe.*

*Loch Treatchachan
in Glen Coe.*

dodged me and Beatrice and Jane Churchill, who were walking about, and was most impertinent when Brown went to tell him to move, which Jane herself had thought of doing. However, he did go away at last, and Brown came back saying he thought there would have been a fight; for when Brown said quite civilly that the Queen wished him to move away, he said he had quite as good a right to remain there as the Queen. To this Brown answered very strongly; upon which the impertinent individual asked, 'Did he know who he was?' and Brown answered he did, and that 'the highest gentlemen in *England* would not dare do what he did, much less a reporter' – and he must move on, or he would give him something more. And the man said, 'Would he dare say that before those other men (all reporters) who were coming up?' And Brown answered 'Yes', he would before 'anybody who did not behave as he ought.' More strong words were used; but the others came up and advised the man to come away quietly, which he finally did. Such conduct ought to be known. We were there nearly an hour, and then began walking down a portion of the steep part.

Loch Leven and the head of Glen Coe.

The parish clergyman, Mr. Stewart, who had followed us up, and who had met us when we arrived at *Ballachulish*, explained the names of the hills, and showed the exact place of the dreadful massacre. He also said that there were many Episcopalians there from the old Jacobite feeling, and also Roman Catholics.

There was seldom frost in the glen, he said, but there was a good deal of snow.

A short distance from where Ossian's cave is shown there is a very small lake called *Loch Treachtan*, through which the *Cona* flows; and at the end of this was a cottage with some cattle and small pieces of cultivated land. We drove down on our return at a great pace. As we came through *Ballachulish* the post-boy suddenly stopped, and a very respectable, stout-looking old Highlander stepped up to the carriage with a small silver quaich, out of which he said Prince Charles had drunk, and also my dearest Albert in 1847, and begged that I would do the same. A table, covered with a cloth and with a bottle on it, was on the other side of the road. I felt I could hardly refuse, and therefore tasted some whisky out of it, which delighted the people who were standing around. His name, we have since heard, is W. A. Cameron.

We drove to the same small pier where we had disembarked, and were rowed over again by two Highlanders in kilts. The evening was so beautiful and calm that the whole landscape was reflected in the lake. There is a high, conical-shaped hill, the commencement of the *Pass of Glencoe*, which is seen best from here; and the range of hills above *Ardgour* and *Corran Ferry* opposite was of the most lovely blue. The whole scene was most beautiful. Three pipers played while we rowed across, and the good people, who were most loyal and friendly, cheered loudly. We re-entered our carriages, and drove off at a quick pace. When we were on the shores of *Loch Eil* again, we stopped (but did not get out) to take tea, having boiled the kettle. The setting sun cast a most glorious light, as yesterday, on *Ben Nevis* and the surrounding hills, which were quite pink, and gave a perfectly crimson hue to the heather on the moor below. The sky was pink and lilac and pale green, and became richer and richer, while the hills in the other direction, over *Fort William*, were of a deep blue. It was wonderfully beautiful, and I was still able to make, or at least begin, a sketch of the effect of it, after we came home at a quarter to seven, from Beatrice's window.

· 11 ·

The Great Glen

WHILST at Inverlochy, Queen Victoria took the opportunity to visit places associated with Bonnie Prince Charlie, in which she recalls feeling a sort of reverence for her Stuart ancestor, even though he attempted to dethrone her great-great-grandfather. It is interesting to note that, at Glenfinnan, she decides that the monument to his memory, at the site of the raising of the standard, is ugly. This is a comment that others since have uttered and one with which I also agree. Although I realize the importance of the monument to Scottish heritage, I think that the only worthwhile reason for a visit is the view of Glen Shiel from the top of it.

Far more impressive is Loch Arkaig a few miles down the Great Glen. To visit, one has to make a detour off the main thoroughfare between Fort William and Inverness, down a minor road which the Queen describes as being the 'Dark Mile'. In summer, the old gnarled trees which populate the slopes of this approach are so heavily laden with foliage as to over-arch the passage completely. This impregnable mantle darkens the road into a tunnel of eerie green dimness in which the lichen-coated stones and moss-eaten barks bewitch a fertile imagination. Unfortunately, the effect is non-existent in the bareness of winter, and all the supernatural atmosphere is lost. However it is still a very pleasant approach to a loch which holds the secret to one of the most intriguing mysteries of the 1745 Rebellion.

Bonnie Prince Charlie was expecting funds to finance the venture and ensure the loyalty of the clans. A French ship actually discharged a large amount of gold on the coast. Observers on the decks of two British warships, which were making a surprise attack, saw the gold being carried away by Jacobite supporters. The money never reached the Prince, however, but did get as far as Loch Arkaig. It was always assumed that the Jacobite supporters, fearing the gold might fall into enemy hands, submerged most of it beneath the grey waters of the loch; and here it probably still lies, awaiting some modern-day treasure-hunter.

Queen Victoria travelled the Great Glen in style, by boat along the Caledonian Canal, and her account of this journey gives a revealing insight into her inquisitive nature. As we now know, her reign is acknowledged as being probably the one of greatest progress in the civilized world, and she was obviously intrigued with these vast technological changes. The canal, designed by Thomas Telford and, where possible, utilizing existing lochs, connects Inverness and Fort William and provides a link between the two coasts. Its construction was no easy task, requiring some 28 lochs including the famous Neptune's Staircase at Banavie which rises, or falls, 64 feet in one mile. In fact, when the canal was first opened in 1822, it still wasn't right and it was closed from 1834–47 for repairs and redesigning. It was intended primarily for commercial traffic, but whilst some fishing boats still use it, it is now predominantly sailed by the vast fleets of pleasure-cruisers. I must admit, it certainly seems an excellent leisurely way to see the geographical beauty of the Glen, though I'm not so sure about crossing Loch Ness, as I've seen some diabolically rough waves for an inland sea. I wouldn't fancy poking my head out of a 30-foot cabin-cruiser in thick fog, to come face to face with Nessie. Though the Queen finished her cruise on this famous stretch of inland water she makes no mention of the alleged presence of the monster. Perhaps the legend was regarded as unsuitable material to impart to so regal a personage.

Visit to Inverlochy, 1873.

Monday, September 15.

... In one valley, which became very narrow after passing a large meadow in which they were making hay, we turned into a narrow sort of defile, with the stream of the *Finnan* flowing on as slowly as an English river, with trees and fir trees on the rocks, and unlike anything I had seen in *Scotland*, and then you come at once on *Loch Shiel* (a freshwater loch), with fine very high rugged hills on either side. It runs down twenty miles.

At the head of the loch stands a very ugly monument to Prince Charles Edward, looking like a sort of lighthouse surmounted by his statue, and surrounded by a wall. Here it was that he landed when he was brought by Macdonald of *Borradale* – whose descendant, now Macdonald of *Glenaladale*, has a house here (the only habitation to be seen) – to wait for the gathering of the clans. When Prince Charlie arrived at the spot where the monument stands, which is close to the loch and opposite to *Glenfinnan* (the road we came going past it and on up a hill to *Arisaig*, twenty-five miles farther on), he found only a dozen peasants, and thought he had been betrayed, and he sat down with his head in his hands. Suddenly the sound of the pipes aroused him, and he saw the clans coming down *Glenfinnan*. Soon after the Macdonalds appeared, and in the midst of a cheering host the Marquis of Tullibardine (Duke of Athole but for his attainder) unfurled the banner of King James. This was in August 1745. In 1746 poor Prince Charles was a fugitive hiding in the mountains on the sides of *Loch Arkaig* and *Loch Shiel.*

Friday, September 12.

. . . As you approach *Achnacarry*, which lies rather low, but is surrounded by very fine trees, the luxuriance of the tangled woods, surmounted by rugged hills, becomes finer and finer till you come to *Loch Arkaig*, a little over half a mile from the house. This is a very lovely loch, reminding one of *Loch Katrine*, especially where there is a little pier, from which we embarked on board a very small but nice screw steamer which belongs to Cameron of *Lochiel.*

He received us (wearing his kilt and plaid) just above the pier, and we all went on board the little steamer. The afternoon was beautiful, and lit up the fine scenery to the greatest advantage. We went about halfway up the *Loch* (which is fourteen miles long), as we had not time to go farther, to the disappointment of Lochiel, who said it grew wilder and wilder higher up. To the left (as we went up) is the deer forest; to the right he has sheep.

Both sides are beautifully wooded all along the lower part of the fine hills which rise on either side, and the trees are all oaks, which Cameron of *Lochiel* said were the 'weed of the country,' and all natural – none were planted. A good many grow up all the hollows and fissures of the hills and rocks. Right ahead, where we turned, was seen a fine conical-shaped hill called *Scour-na-nat*, and to the left *Glenmally*, to the north *Muir Logan*, and *Guisach* and *Gerarnan* on either side. Before we came to the turning we three had our tea, which was very refreshing. I tried to sketch a little, but the sun shone so strongly that I could not do much. . . .

Glenfinnan in Glen Shiel.

It was, as General Ponsonby observed afterwards, a striking scene. 'There was Lochiel,' as he said, 'whose great-grand-uncle had been the real moving cause of the uprising of 1745 – for without him Prince Charles would not have made the attempt – showing your Majesty (whose great-great-grand-father he had striven to dethrone) the scenes made historical by Prince Charlie's wanderings. It was a scene one could not look on unmoved.'

Yes; and *I* feel a sort of reverence in going over these scenes in this most beautiful country, which I am proud to call my own, where there was such devoted loyalty to the family of my ancestors – for Stuart blood is in my veins, and I am *now* their representative, and the people are as devoted and loyal to me as they were to that unhappy race.

We landed at the little pier, but walked over the small bridges (the carriages following) – on which a piper was play-ing – a few hundred yards to the gate (on the side opposite to that by which we came), where we got into the carriages again. We drove through a beautiful road called the *Dark Mile* – dark from the number of very fine trees which overhang it, while on the left it is overshadowed by beetling rocks with a rich tangled undergrowth of bracken and heather, etc. The heather grows very richly and fully in these parts, and in thick tufts. We saw here the cave in which Prince Charles Edward was hid for a week.

Tuesday, September 16.

. . . We drove to *Banavie*, where a good many people were assembled, and stepped on board the steamer which was on the *Caledonian Canal*. Here were Lord and Lady Abinger, whom I thanked very much for their kindness. I left an illus-trated copy of my book and prints of Albert's and my portraits

Loch Arkaig.

The Dark Mile.

*Ben Nevis from
Corpach.*

at *Inverlochy* for Lord Abinger. She is an American lady from the *Southern States*, a Miss Macgruder, and they have five children, of whom one only is a boy. They left the steamer, and we began moving. The steamer is called the 'Gondolier'. It is built on the same principle as the one we had on *Loch Lomond*, with a fine large cabin with many windows, almost a deck cabin (though it is down one flight of steps), which extends through the ship with seats below, open at the sides far forward. In this large cabin sixty-two people can dine. We remained chiefly on deck. We steamed gently along under the road by which we had driven from *Gairlochy* and *Achnacarry*, Lochiel's to the left or west, and Lord Abinger's to the right. *Ben Nevis*, unfortunately, was hid in mist, and the top invisible, which we hear is very generally the case.

We came to one loch, and then shortly afterwards to *Gairlochy*, after which you enter *Loch Lochy*. The *Caledonian Canal* is a very wonderful piece of engineering, but travelling by it is very tedious. At each lock people crowded up close to the steamer. As the river rises from *Banavie* to *Loch Oich* (which succeeds *Loch Lochy*), the canal has to raise the vessels up to that point, and again to lower them from *Loch Oich* to *Inverness*. The vessel, on entering the lock from the higher level, is enclosed by the shutting of the gates. The sluices of the lower gates are raised by small windlasses (it was amusing to see the people, including the crew of the steamer, who went on shore to expedite the operation, which is not generally done, run round and round to move these windlasses), and holes are thus opened at the bottom of the lower gates, through which the water flows till the water in the lock sinks to the lowest level. The lower gates are then opened, as the water is on the lowest level, while the upper gates keep back the water above. The same process raises the ships in the lock which ascend. About five or six feet can be raised or depressed in this manner at each lock. (I have copied this from an account General Ponsonby wrote for me.)

As we entered *Loch Lochy*, which looked beautiful, we saw where *Loch Arkaig* lay, though it was hid from us by high ground. The hills which rise from *Loch Lochy* are excellent pasture for sheep, but the lower parts are much wooded. After eight miles' sail on *Loch Lochy* we came to *Loch Oich*, which is entered by another lock at *Laggan*. Here Mr. and Mrs. Ellice (who is a first cousin of the Greys) were waiting, and came on board. They had wished me to get out and drive round their fine place, *Invergarry*, to rejoin the steamer at the next lock,

Noble, the Queen's collie.

but I declined, preferring to remain quietly on board, though the process of going through the locks is slow and necessarily tedious. It is nervous work to steer, for there is hardly a foot to spare on either side. Mrs. Ellice went on shore again, having given us some fine grapes, but Mr. Ellice remained on board till the next lock, *Cullochy*. A road much shaded runs along the side of the loch, and here we passed the small monument by its side, put over the well into which a number of heads of some of the MacDonalds, who had murdered two of their kinsmen of *Keppoch*, were thrown after they had been killed in revenge for this act, by order of MacDonald of the Isles. It was erected in 1812. We next came to the old ruined castle of *Invergarry*, embosomed in trees, close to which, but not in sight, is Mr. Ellice's new house. He has an immense deal of property here on both sides. The hills rise high, and one conically shaped one called *Ben Tigh* towers above the rest. At *Cullochy* Mr. Ellice left the steamer. Mr. Brewster, formerly Lord Chancellor of *Ireland* and nearly eighty years old, was standing on the shore here. Francie and one of the policemen got out with good Noble, and walked to meet us again at *Fort Augustus*. While we were stopping to go through one of the locks, a poor woman came and brought us a jug of milk and oat-cake, which with their usual hospitality the country people constantly offer.

After this, and at about ten minutes past twelve, Beatrice, Jane Churchill, and I went below and had some hot luncheon. The people from the locks looked down upon us, but it was unavoidable. We had now reached *Fort Augustus*, where there was again some delay and a great many people, and where

The Caledonian Canal.

there was a triumphal arch. Here on this very day thirty-six years ago my beloved Albert passed, and he saw poor Macdonald the Jäger here, and took a liking to him from his appearance, and, being in want of a Jäger, inquired after him and engaged him. He was keeper to Lord Digby and Colonel Porter then, and brought some game for dearest Albert from them, and Albert was greatly struck by his good looks. He was very handsome, especially in the kilt, which he habitually wore.

There had been a heavy shower, but it was over when we came up on deck again. We entered *Loch Ness* here. It is twenty-four miles long, and broad, the banks wooded, with many pretty places on them.

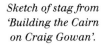

Sketch of stag from 'Building the Cairn on Craig Gowan'.

Loch Ness.

Loch Lochy.

· 12 ·

The North of Scotland

IN all the years of her reign, and in all her excursions to her beloved Scotland, Queen Victoria made only two journeys further north than Inverness and even these did not enter into the most outlying districts of her Scottish empire.

The first of these was to Dunrobin on the east coast, where she spent several days at the castle. She did not venture too far from the grounds though she did go as far as Loch Brora, around which is an area boasting the earliest coal-mining in Scotland, dating from 1529. It was also from this area that some of the first settlers for New Zealand left the British Isles. The loch, unlike many of its counterparts, is not surrounded by really dramatic mountains, but nevertheless it is a very photogenic stretch of water; I can easily understand why the Queen was enchanted by its qualities and spent some time sketching on its banks. I was quite fortunate to arrive at 6.30 one spring morning and was thus able to watch the distinctive warm quality of a post-dawn sun accentuate the redness of the Carroll Rock, which contrasted vividly with the blue cloudless sky.

I made a foray into Golspie Glen which runs inland behind the castle, just a few miles back down the coast. This glen has a series of well-planned paths and bridges which meander along it and up and down its fairly steep slopes, providing a superb walk past its rocky little outcrops and over its gentle cascades. Amongst the plants can be found a wide variety of mosses and lichens, displaying a great many shades of colour.

The expedition to Loch Maree in Torridon took the Queen to a different world entirely, a world which it is hard to believe is only about 60 miles away, across on the west coast. The terrain is far more hostile and wild, and inhabited by pine marten, fox, wildcat and eagle. Part of it belongs to the Beinn Eighe nature reserve, where fossils have been found dating back some 600 million years.

The rock formations are one of the most interesting aspects of the area, and they certainly impressed the Queen, especially the terracing of Liathach deep in Glen Torridon. Personally I found the massive stone boulders littering the shores of Loch Maree a far more exciting proposition visually; the textures in some cases seemed to resemble the hides of elephants. Even in the height of a tourist summer season this area remains relatively remote; the railway reaches no nearer than the tiny station of Achnasheen, just as it did at the time of the royal visit, though the old single-track road running parallel with the line is presently being widened. In my opinion, this desecration, which is being repeated in many of the more rustic parts of Scotland, does nothing to help the primitive charm of the Highlands and, whilst many argue that it is necessary for progress, I wonder what Queen Victoria would have made of it, considering she found inaccessibility one of the major attractions.

Expedition to Loch Maree, 1877.

Wednesday, September 12, 1877.

. . . The twenty miles drive from here, through a desolate, wild, and perfectly uninhabited country, was beautiful, though unfortunately we had heavy showers. The first part winds along *Loch Rusque* (Gaelic Chriosg), a long narrow loch, with hills very like those at the *Spital* and at *Glen Muich* rising on either side. Looking back you see the three high peaks of *Scour-na-Vuillin.* The road continues along another small loch; and then from the top of the hill you go down a very grand pass called *Glen Dochart.* Here *Loch Maree* came in view most beautifully. Very shortly after this you come upon the loch, which is grand and romantic. We changed horses at *Kinlochewe*, a small inn, near to which is a shooting-lodge, which was for some time rented by Lady Waterpark's son-in-law, Mr. Clowes, and he and his wife used to live there a good

Loch Rusque.

Maree stones.

deal. They are now living near *Gairloch*, at *Flowerdale*, another shooting-lodge of Sir Kenneth Mackenzie.

The drive along the lochside, for ten miles to the hotel of *Loch Maree*, is beautiful in the extreme. The hills to the right, as you go from *Kinlochewe*, are splendid – very high and serrated, with wood at the base of some of them. One magnificent hill towers above the rest, and is not unlike the *Pilatus* in shape, seen as it is from our hotel, just as the *Pilatus* is seen from the *Pension Wallis*. The windings of the road are beautiful, and afford charming glimpses of the lake, which is quite locked in by the overlapping mountains. There are trees, above and below it, of all kinds, but chiefly birch, pine, larch, and alder, with quantities of high and mostly beautiful heather and bracken growing luxuriantly, high rocks surmounting the whole. Here and there a fine Scotch fir, twisted, and with a stem and head like a stone-pine, stands out on a rocky projection into the loch, relieved against the blue hills as in some Italian view. Part of the way the road emerges altogether from the trees, and passes by a mass of huge piled-up and tumbled-about stones, which everywhere here are curiously marked, almost as though they were portions of a building, and have the appearance of having been thrown

Loch Maree.

about by some upheaving of the earth. We had several heavy showers, which produced a most brilliant rainbow, with the reflection of a second, quite perfect. Then it quite cleared up, and the sky was radiant with the setting sun, which gave a crimson hue to all the hills, and lit up *Ben Sleach* just as I remember having seen it light up Ben *Nevis* and the surrounding hills at *Inverlochy*. . . .

Saturday, September 15.

. . . At *Kinlochewe* we turned up to the right by the stream of *Garry*, mountains towering up as we advanced, like mighty giants, and coming one by one and unexpectedly into view. To the left we passed a pretty, small loch, called *Loch Clare*, which runs back into a wooded glen at the foot of high hills. Sir Ivor Guest has a shooting-lodge near, and you can just see a small house amongst the trees.

Soon after this the grand, wild, savage-looking, but most beautiful and picturesque *Glen of Torridon* opened upon us, with the dark mural precipices of that most extraordinary mountain *Ben Liughach*, which the people pronounce *Liarach*. We were quite amazed as we drove below it. The mountains here rise so abruptly from their base that they seem much higher than our *Aberdeenshire* mountains, although, excepting *Ben Sleach* (3,216 feet) and a few others, the hills are not of any remarkable height, and the level of the country or land itself is barely a hundred feet above the sea, whereas Balmoral is eight hundred feet to begin with. All the hills about *Loch Maree* and this glen, and elsewhere in this neighbourhood, are very serrated and rocky. *Ben Liarach* is most peculiar from its being so dark, and the rocks like terraces one above the other, or like fortifications and pillars – most curious; the glen itself is very flat, and the mountains rise very abruptly on either side.

Visit to Dunrobin, 1872.

Tuesday, September 10.

. . . At half-past ten got on my pony Maggie, Annie and Jane Churchill walking, and went to see the *Golspie Burn Falls*. We made two mistakes before we got right. We went out by the usual approach down to the mill, and past the mill under the great arch for the railway, over some very rough stones in the river, and then along a path in the wood full of hazel bushes

Glen Torridon.

and trees of all kinds, till the glen narrows very much, and we came to a wooden bridge, where I got off and walked to the head of the falls—over several foot-bridges, along a small path overhung by high rocks and full of vegetation. It is extremely pretty, reminding me of *Corriemulzie*, only on a much smaller scale. I mounted my pony again, and rode home the same way about twelve. Very warm. We had a few drops of rain, but it remained very fine all day.

At ten minutes to four started with the two children and Annie Sutherland in my waggonette for *Loch Brora*, which is nine miles off. We drove past the stables out on the main *Caithness* road, through the small fishing village of *Brora*, where all the people were out, and where they had raised a triumphal arch and decorated the village with heather. We turned sharp to the left, and came into a wild moor country, stopping for a moment at a place where one of the new coal mines which the Duke has found is being worked. One of these, near the sea, we had passed on Sunday. Then on, till we came very soon to the commencement of *Loch Brora*, which is seven miles in length, very narrow at first, and out of which the *Brora* flows into the sea. The hills heighten as the loch widens, and to the left as we drove along the *Carrol Hill* rises

*Liathach from
Glen Torridon.*

*The burn
in Golspie Glen.*

Loch Brora.

very finely with bold rocks up above the loch. An hour's drive took us to the Fishing Cottage, a small wooden house, built like a châlet, which is just off the road, on the grass. Here we got out. The Duke drove his break, four horses in hand. They had never been together before, and it was not easy to drive them, for the road is full of turnings and rather narrow. Lord Granville sat on the box with him; and Constance Westminster, Jane Churchill, the Duchess de San Arpino (who had just arrived, and is a great friend of the Duchess) and Lady Granville were inside, and two grooms sitting behind. The three young ladies, and Mr. Collins, and Colonel Ponsonby followed in the waggonette. They had started before us, but we caught them up at *Brora*. MacAlister had broiled some fish and got tea ready for us in a very small room upstairs in this little cottage, where there was a fire. I had my coffee. We ladies and Leopold all squeezed into this room. It was a very merry tea. The tea over, we all went down to see a haul of fish. It was very successful; quantities of brilliantly red char, trout, and two salmon, both of which had to be put back again. After this haul I went up and sat sketching on the balcony while there were several more hauls, which Macdonald the keeper superintended, and some walked, and others rowed. The view, looking towards the *Carrol Hill*, was lovely, and the colouring beautiful.

The ladies and gentlemen rowed across, having sent the carriages round, but I preferred *terra firma*, and drove round the loch to where the *Black-Water* runs into *Loch Brora*, and is literally black; we drove over it. The Duchess told us that there was a fine drive into a wild country up that glen. We drove along the loch side, really a beautiful drive, under the *Carrol Rock* or *Hill*, through the *Carrol Wood*; the trees seem to grow remarkably well there. We saw some deer on the very top of the hills. As we drove along the loch, some high hills were seen rising up behind the low ones on the opposite side, one of which, called *Ben Arlmin*, is in the Duke's nearest deer-forest.

· 13 ·

Victoria's Footsteps

THE most pleasing aspect for those readers who want to follow quite literally in Queen Victoria's footsteps is that, for the most part, the walks I have chosen remain relatively unchanged from the walks she knew. The scenery is almost as the Queen saw and described it – except for the tarmacked roads, which must be an improvement on the rutted tracks of Her Majesty's time and actually provide much easier access for any royal-journey follower!

If you don't want to walk, then you can follow many routes by car, stopping as desired to visit and view the scenes Queen Victoria described. Queen's View, Glen Coe or Melrose Abbey all make highly enjoyable excursions for the car-bound tourist.

And if you can be persuaded to take a short walk away from your vehicle – on flat, albeit not totally concrete, terrain – then certain of these excursions are along roads which are of good quality for some distance before they become either prohibited or impassable! Into this category, fall the excursions up Glen Nevis (near Fort William), Glen Shira (near Inveraray) and, by payment of a small permission charge, Glen Tilt (near Pitlochry) as far as Forest Lodge.

These side roads are marked on most road-maps and are, in any event, surprisingly well signposted. True, they *can* be enjoyed from the comfort of a car but it would be a shame not to take advantage of the landscape and – following Queen Victoria's example – discover your own hidden gems of nature: such as the Falls of Golspie (above Dornoch) and Bruar (above Pitlochry). Both of these waterfalls are well signposted from the road and have car parking-facilities.

In addition, the owners have laid out an excellent trail of good paths and bridges to enable you to reach the best vantage points. However, by virtue of their location, a certain amount of hard walking is necessary to reach your destination. The designers of the paths have endeavoured to make the 'climbs' run along the routes of least resistance and all should be within the capability of most people between the ages of 7 and 77 years (and indeed some even older).

The only two suggestions I would make are: firstly, whilst the waterfall paths are safe and, where necessary, cordoned off with very stout railings, they are still potentially dangerous and great care must be taken when walking with children, especially those of an exceptionally inquisitive or daredevil nature; secondly, all the terrain so far mentioned can be traversed easily with sensible footwear but trainers may prove to have insufficiently stable grip in light mud, wet leaves or on damp rock, all of which can still be encountered at the height of a summer drought.

The excursions in the last category are the most exciting because each one goes into the wild Scottish Highlands where you can only go on foot unless, like the Queen, you go by pony. Nevertheless, having made the trek, I believe that there are sections of the route where even a pony would have difficulty if it had a rider aboard! The four walks which are described and mapped below *do* have sections at their beginnings which make excellent strolls for the ordinary well-shod tourist who wants a taste of this wilderness.

Complete excursions, however, should only be undertaken by reasonably fit and experienced walkers, as all involve some climbing and are several miles in length. They should not be attempted without correct footwear and, even in summer, a backpack of spare clothing and provisions.

In addition, though most of the ways are on identifiable paths it is advisable for at least one member of the party to be proficient with map and compass – as weather conditions can change rapidly. All the routes are shown and described as taken by Queen Victoria but they can of course be done in reverse!

Glen Builg/Glen Avon.

This route can be attempted from either direction. Its completion requires either two cars or a non-walking driver.

Start almost opposite Balmoral Castle entrance, take the B976 towards Gairnshiel Lodge, and begin to climb. The road winds for about a mile then turns sharply right. Here, to your left, is a very obvious Land-Rover track. This is the point where you should leave your vehicle. For a pick-up point, drive into Tomintoul village on the A939/B9008 and, instead of turning right towards Grantown-on-Spey, take the left turn signposted Delnabo.

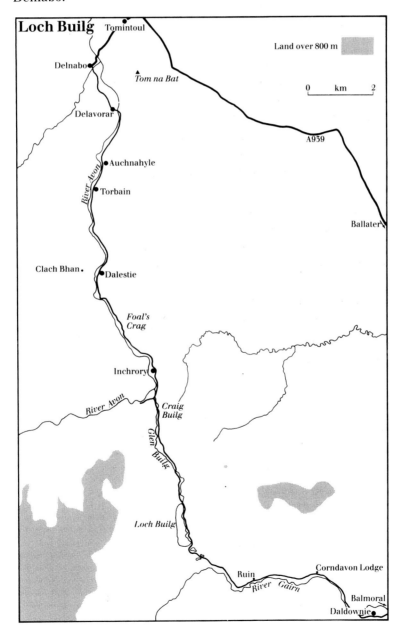

Follow this road through Delnabo, until you reach a sign which tells you that you are about to enter the Private Inchrory Estate. Leave your pick-up vehicle here. *Do not* attempt to go further because the road is gated and padlocked a short distance beyond this sign.

Most of this walk is on relatively flat ground, on good Land-Rover tracks. There are, however, a couple of fords to cross either side of Loch Builg, which are impossible to negotiate in a completely dry state. I waded barefoot through the water but it was in late April and in winter months some other preventive measures (such as plastic bags) may be advisable.

The most difficult section of this walk is around Loch Builg where at times the track becomes barely visible, disappearing into a morass of mud of seemingly superglue consistency! Keeping the loch to your left, a relatively solid way can be picked out, and the Land-Rover track is easily regained – just before the loch disgorges into Glen Builg. The way is obvious from here, as it eventually joins the Avon and a particularly good road winds along the bottom of its gorge.

As you approach Inchrory Lodge with the Builg Burn to your left, you will see a man-made bridge which leads off left to reach Loch Avon in the heart of the Cairngorms. Whilst this diversion is not part of the walk, it is worth following this track for a couple of hundred yards to view the Linn of Avon to your right.

Glen Callater/Glas Maol/Caenlochan.

Arrive along the A93 from Braemar towards the Cairnwell Ski Centre. The valley along which you travel will begin to narrow, and you will see on your right a house and on your left a car park. There is a bridleway signpost to Loch Callater. Your car can be left here if you intend to walk to Caenlochan and return.

The walk can be shortened, however, by adhering more strictly to the itinerary of Queen Victoria, in which case your finishing point will be further up the A93. If using two cars, or if you can persuade your poor driver to read a book while you have a jolly time on the mountain, arrange for the pick-up car to continue along until, as the road begins to climb quite abruptly towards the pass summit, it reaches a car-park immediately off the road to the left.

Your driver could always visit the Cairnwell for coffee in the cafeteria, before taking the chairlift to a summit a mere fifty feet lower than that you will have struggled all day to achieve.

The walk progresses on a good but quite boring Land-Rover

track along Glen Callater, until you reach the beautiful Loch Callater. At this point, take the track, which first skirts the right-hand shore for a short way, then strikes off very steeply, right up the mountainside.

About half-way up, this track narrows into a path which peters out completely a short distance from a steep corrie, into which you can look to view Loch Kander. There is nothing now to show you the way but your map-reading capabilities and common-sense. Put your back to the corrie and head for the nearest visible high point. One modern pointer to assist you to the summit of Carn an Tuirc is that below and to your right can be seen a ski tow.

The ground at the summit falls away sharply in all directions except that which you have come. Looking south (to your left) as you approach the summit, you will see, across a gulley and a spur, an almost sheer rock wall in the distance. Beyond this is your next summit. Here commonsense must take command as you skirt the gulley and make for this summit across the ground of least slope. Unfortunately, with no path, you must rely on your own discretion here, rather than on any definite instruction I can give you.

Breathe a sigh of relief at the summit of Cairn of Claise, for here you rediscover a path! Follow it to a T-junction, where you turn left and cross the shoulder of Glas Maol. As you begin to descend, slightly away from the summit, follow your natural instincts of preservation and slow down because Caenlochan soon presents itself – very immediately and almost under your left foot. It was somewhere along here that Queen Victoria held her picnic party. The view along this path is spectacular, to say the least.

Now return the way you came, not forgetting to take the path off right to the summit of Cairn of Claise; after which the return to Carn an Tuirc over unmarked ground again demand common-sense.

If the weather is bad on leaving Claise, stay well clear of the drop into Garbh Choire on your left. At Carn an Tuirc, descend as safely as possible to the ski tow, and thence to the path which will take you to the old military bridge by the A93 and the welcome sight of your waiting vehicle.

If visibility is poor and the ski tow invisible make the trek back to the road the long way round *via* the floor of Glen Callater.

This route is long and strenuous. Some of it is also pathless; and because these parts of the walk go very near to dangerous slopes and precipices, I would advise against undertaking it in adverse conditions.

Lochnagar/Loch Muick/Dubh Loch

The ascent of Lochnagar described by Queen Victoria is that marked **A** on the map – but it is not the one which I used!

My reason for preferring an approach from Loch Muick is as follows. A strong walker can take in all the main locations described in the passages I have chosen in one long and enjoyable day. Three of the locations can also be visited by non-experienced hillwalkers, with the added advantage that the routes are circular, beginning and ending at the car park at Loch Muick.

The car park is well signposted from the main A93. The walk around Loch Muick is not strenuous and is within the capabilities of most people. For the most part it follows a well-surfaced track although this does become a muddy path at the far end of the loch. The round of the loch is best achieved in an anti-clockwise direction. This is also the best way should you intend to visit Glas-allt Falls and Dubh Loch: then a return can be made the same way, avoiding the worst of the path at the far end of the loch.

On passing the warden's hut walk straight on along the track until you see a path which meanders round the head of the loch towards a boat-house on the far shore. Take this path and regain the main track. Follow on until the forests surrounding the Glas-allt Shiel are before you. Here, take the track which deviates right, high into the forests, rather than staying on the roadway.

This area is still occasionally used by the Royal Family, and the reason the path skirts the back of the forest rather than keeping to the shoreline is to ensure their privacy – which should be respected. To visit the Falls of Glas-allt, take a path left which crosses a wall. This path is after the wooden bridge which crosses the Glas-allt Burn as it flows into the forest. From here it is but a short steep climb to view the falls.

For a visit to the Dubh Loch, continue on the path out of the forest and back to the loch side. The path you now require leaves this main path a short distance along on your right, and climbs until it reaches a narrow defile giving excellent views of the loch.

For those who wish to embark on the whole round, instead of going straight on after passing the warden's hut at the beginning of the previous walk, turn to the right and make for the buildings of Alt-na-Giuthasach. Pass behind these and continue up the track signposted to Lochnagar. This track (**C** on map) continues to rise until, after veering right, it becomes obvious that it will soon begin to descend into the Dee Valley.

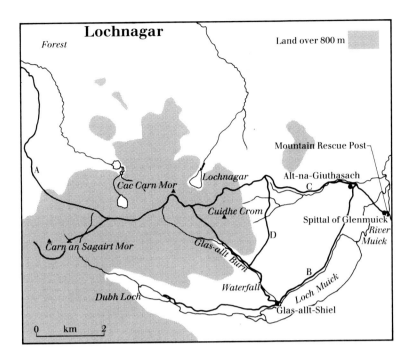

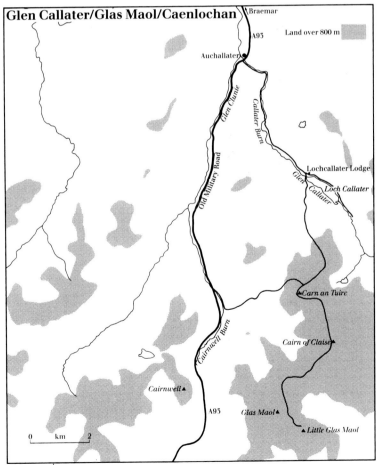

Take the path which departs left and which is the obvious way to Lochnagar. The track eventually narrows into a zigzag way on scree, which brings you to the summit ridge.

A short worthwhile detour is to strike out 'vertically' from the beginning of the zigzags, up to the col above. This will eventually bring you to a superb view of Lochnagar and the vertical precipices of Black and Red Spouts.

Back on the main 'path', follow on as the path will eventually take you all the way around the rim of the corrie, affording breathtaking views. In adverse conditions, great care is required. Bear in mind that in snow what looks like solid ground may be a cornice, not too firmly attached to the solid ground you left several feet back. (In the conditions I experienced on my photographic expedition, only the completely insane would continue on this route to the summit!)

I returned down the path, almost to the main track (C) where a path branches off right. This makes a pleasant way to the Falls of Glas-allt for those who have climbed to this point, and want to climb no further. It makes a pleasant alternative – with differing views – to returning the way you came, and is mainly flat and downhill all the way. In parts the path is hard to follow and does occasionally melt into the heather, and the beginning of it can be difficult to find.

Eventually you will come to the main path, from summit to loch side, which follows the Glas-allt Burn – the path you would have been on had you continued to the top of Lochnagar in the first place. Turn left. The path seems to continue down both sides of the burn but it is advisable to cross it now. I didn't, and had to retrace my steps because the water became impassable as I tramped ever closer to the head of the falls.

From here the path is safe and clear all the way to the forest below. Great care must be taken on the very steep section down the side of the Glas-allt. When reaching the bridge (previously mentioned on the main round of the loch), either turn left to the car park or, if still full of surplus energy, turn right and follow the directions given for Dubh Loch!

Ben Macdui (Including a View of Loch Avon).

Of all the excursions made by Queen Victoria this is my favourite. It is for the serious walker, being a strenuous full-day expedition with a 3500-foot ascent and 12-mile distance. Whilst normally on paths – if attempted in good conditions – an adequate map-reading/compass capability is required. For even in apparently good

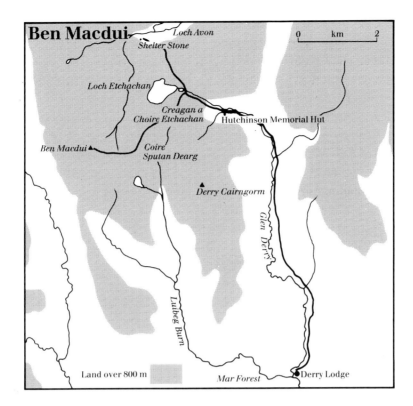

conditions, the Cairngorm plateau upon which you will walk, can become a featureless dazzling landscape in snow.

In addition you will enter an area notorious for its rapid weather changes, which include blizzards at the height of summer. Remember, many walkers have wandered blindly after being caught in instant storms, only to perish of cold or stumble over a precipice. No warning can be too severe. There is danger even on the lower reaches of Glen Derry where the lack of tree or rock shelter resulted in a group of young soldiers freezing to death one spring not too long ago.

Be adequately equipped. That seemingly cumbersome excess of clothing and provisions could so easily save your life.

Drive to the Linn of Dee (signposted out of Braemar), and continue round to the car park. Your starting point is further along this road, but vehicles left haphazardly on the grass verges make the place look untidy! Follow the Land-Rover track signposted to Glen Derry all the way to Derry Lodge. At this point, you can either bear right, continuing on the track, or cross the bridge and follow the path through the bottom of Glen Derry. The choice is yours but – if you want to stay clean and dry at the expense of a small amount of uphill legwork then stick to the track! They both end up at the same point where, passing through the deer-proof fence, the path now continues along the upper reaches of the glen. Take the left branch where the path forks, otherwise you will end up at the Ford of Avon and that means you will have overshot your approach by about two miles . . . cross the footbridge and climb until you reach the Hutchison memorial hut.

Provided that you had an early start, this is a very good place to stop to prepare yourself for the steepest climb of the day. For a little light relief take a look at the visitor's book in the hut which displays superb examples of the particularly dry wit of the seasoned walkers who use such spartan accommodation: for example, the wag who called especially on Christmas Day and was disappointed to find the tenants 'Out to Lunch' or the earlier guest who compliments the 'accommodation' but bemoans the fact that the central heating needs an overhaul. (There isn't any.)

Fully refreshed, continue on the path upwards which, though becoming ever steeper and harder, affords magnificent sideways views of Corrie Etchachan. On reaching the col, your drained batteries should be instantly recharged by the superb vista before you; of Loch Etchachan and its almost sheer rock-face with the plateau above and beyond.

Your path continues along the left shore, rising less abruptly than the face, and at less of an incline than the path out of Glen Derry which you have just left. To take in the view of Loch Avon with Cairngorm beyond, detour across the gently rising ground to your right, away from Etchachan on a well-defined path.

Back on the trail to Ben Macdui, you will rise from Loch Etchachan on another one of those screes which will bring you perilously close to the rim of Coire Sputan Dearg on your left (across which you can view Derry Cairngorm). The path veers slightly, left continuing the ascent to the summit of Macdui. As there is no discernible path until half-way down into the glen, if your intention is to return by Queen Victoria's route into Glen Lui, I would suggest returning to this point to make the descent right down the rim of this corrie until the path is reached.

Follow the path down, staying left along the glen floor until you reach Derry Lodge and retrace the first part of your walk back to the car. The alternative route down from Ben Macdui is by the path to Coire Sputan Dearg and then off right over Derry Cairngorm, instead of descending to Loch Etchachan.

On a clear day you will be able to see the route from the corrie top. There are no paths, however, and any descent into Glen Lui or Derry from this mountain or the spur of Carn Crom is over very steep terrain or precipices and is *not* recommended.

Index